1 0 S T E P S T O

Successful Change Management

1 0 STEPS TO

Successful Change Management

George Vukotich, PhD

ASTD PRESS
Alexandria, Virginia

ASTD Press is an internationally renowned source of insightful and practical information on workplace learning and performance topics, including training basics, evaluation and return-on-investment, instructional systems development, e-learning, leadership, and career development.

Ordering information: Books published by ASTD Press can be purchased by visiting ASTD's website at store.astd.org or by calling 800.628.2783 or 703.683.8100.

Library of Congress Control Number: 2010917211
ISBN-10: 1-56286-753-9
ISBN-13: 978-1-56286-753-9

ASTD Press Editorial Staff:
Director: Anthony Allen
Manager, ASTD Press: Larry Fox
Project Manager, Content Acquisition: Justin Brusino
Senior Associate Editor: Tora Estep
Associate Editor: Ashley McDonald
Editorial Assistant: Stephanie Castellano
Copyeditor: Melinda Masson
Indexer: Abella Publishing Services, LLC
Interior Design and Production: Abella Publishing Services, LLC
Cover Design: Steve Fife

Printed by Versa Press, Inc., East Peoria, IL, www.versapress.com

Let's face it, most people spend their days in chaotic, fast-paced, time- and resource-strained organizations. Finding time for just one more project, assignment, or even learning opportunity—no matter how career enhancing or useful—is difficult to imagine. The *10 Steps* series is designed for today's busy professional who needs advice and guidance on a wide array of topics ranging from project management to people management, from business strategy to decision making and time management, from leading effective meetings to researching and creating a compelling presentation. Each book in this ASTD series promises to take its readers on a journey to solid understanding, with practical application the ultimate destination. This is truly a just-tell-me-what-to-do-now series. You will find action-driven language teamed with examples, worksheets, case studies, and tools to help you quickly implement the right steps and chart a path to your own success. The *10 Steps* series will appeal to a broad business audience from middle managers to upper-level management. Workplace learning and human resource professionals, along with other professionals seeking to improve their value proposition in their organizations, will find these books a great resource.

C O N T E N T S

PREFACE

Change will happen. Whether it's personal, political, or economic, there is no stopping it. Individuals who fail to adapt become less valued, and organizations that fail to change are not around for very long. Just look at the stars of yesterday or the people you went to school with or worked with a few years back. Often the high school star stopped growing, and unfortunately, their fame ended in high school. Look at someone you have worked with in the past and ask yourself: Are they continuing to change and better themselves, or are they living off some accomplishment from years ago? Look at the Fortune 500 over a ten-year period of time and you can see that roughly half of the companies listed are gone, but also keep in mind that this means there are new ones that have taken their place. Why? It all has to do with the ability to successfully manage change.

Seeing opportunities and understanding threats, along with knowing strengths and weaknesses, are the starting points for change. Having the capability to react proactively rather than reactively gives us an upper hand as the world turns. Knowing why and asking "what if" allows us to be ready and prepared to take advantage of what is going on around us.

My hope is that the information here gives you some tools and insights you can use to successfully manage the change taking place around you.

A number of individuals have made this book possible. It started with my taking over as the department chair of the graduate program in training and development at Roosevelt University in Chicago and looking for ways to do something new and better to make a difference and help the school and program become a recognized leader in the field. I'd like to think it was a proactive approach to change rather than the fear of losing my job, but it led to working with Dean Smith, a visionary at ASTD, who was also looking for a way to make a difference in what he was doing. Together we created the first university/ASTD partnership that led to what was, at that time, known as the Higher Education Affiliate Program, which has benefited thousands of individuals and moved the field ahead with a creative and innovative approach to having universities and professional associations work together. Dean, thank you.

I'd also like to thank those who have followed Dean at ASTD, and my colleagues at Roosevelt University and in the field of training and development for their support in making this happen.

Finally, I thank my family for their support and for allowing me the quiet time needed to get this work done.

It all comes together as a great network brings support and helps to make things happen. Thank you.

George Vukotich, PhD

I N T R O D U C T I O N

Successfully managing change will always be important. As the pace of change continues to increase, the skills needed to know how to change to be better, faster, and cheaper will increase in importance. Whether the change is based on new technological capability (just look at what the Internet has done), advances in healthcare and the quality of life, organizational changes (mergers and acquisitions, downsizing, outsourcing, off-shoring, start-up), or changes in geo-political positions around the world, those that can adapt and be in front of the change curve will have the most success.

Managing, and in some cases, creating change offers opportunities and challenges. The key is to understand what is happening, minimize the risk that goes with it, and take advantage of the opportunities it can bring. Developing a skill set and building a network of the right individuals with the right skills can make a difference. In this book, we will give you some ideas that will help.

Throughout my time in working with organizations, I have had the opportunity to be involved in a number of organizational change efforts, many of which have had a major impact on the organizations and individuals in them. What I have seen is that those who plan and deal with change—rather than complain about it—end up moving on faster and being more successful in the long run. Others complain, are often miserable, and bring down the morale of those around them.

I have worked in consulting, corporate, and educational environments, and I spent time in the military. Regardless of the environment or organization, certain characteristics and skills stand out with individuals who are successful in making change happen. Those who take advantage of and make the most of the change around them do better, are more successful, and are happier about life in general. Our goal here is to help you learn about and develop some skills to allow you to make the most of and take advantage of the situations and change processes you become involved in.

What You'll Find in This Book

This book is written for individuals facing change and wanting to make change happen. Each step has content and specific tips intended to help evaluate and take advantage of the change process. We go through a 10-step approach that has been developed over the years. Each step links to scanning, planning, and enacting, giving you tips and tools you can use to be more successful.

You will find this book to be a direct resource you can use, not a book to file away in a drawer or hide on a shelf. It is not an exhaustive study of change, although you will see examples; rather, it is meant to be a quick read with steps that can be implemented easily and contain the essential keys to team success. You can read it as 10 steps that build on each other, or you can go directly to the step that interests you and will help solve a particular problem. In the end, the goal is to provide you with some insights, tools, and techniques to put you ahead of the change curve.

In short, here are the 10 steps leading to successful change management:

Step 1: Understand Change. Change happens for a number of reasons, in a number of areas, and in a number of ways. From a corporate perspective, on average over any ten-year period of time, half the companies on the Fortune 500 list fall off. This is not all bad. The good news is that 250 new companies take their place. The companies that fell off the list either did not change or changed too slowly to keep up with others. The new companies found ways to change and be more effective. Whether you look at it by industry, by changes in the world economy, or by innovations in technology, change happens. From a personal perspective, we have all seen individuals rise to be recognized by the media as successes one year and quickly fall into obscurity the next. The key to success is being prepared for change and, in some cases, making change happen rather than having it happen to you.

Step 2: Assess the Impact of Change. Being able to see how change can impact an organization and its individuals makes a difference in whether an organization thrives, survives, or ceases to exist. The dynamics and interaction in a range of areas from competition to technology to changes in customer taste make it imperative that we accurately assess the impact of change on our organization. What to start doing, continue doing, and stop doing determines our value to those we serve. Understanding the environment in which an organization exists and what it takes to be successful is key to not only surviving but thriving through change.

Step 3: Assemble a Change Management Team. It takes having the right people with the right skills—and even more important, the right attitude—to make change happen. Once the goals of the change initiative have been identified, a team needs to be put together. Identifying the roles and tasks to execute on the change strategy is the starting point. Finding and recruiting the right people to be part of the team are important factors in the level of success that will be achieved. This step looks at the characteristics of building an effective change team.

Step 4: Build a Vision for Change. Someone has an idea of how things can be better, or someone realizes that if things stay the way they are, the organization will no longer be able to exist. They look to see what the future could bring. They understand the environment they work in, the competition they face, and the reality of what is and, more importantly, of what could be. They have ideas. They see how things can be different and better, and they come up with a vision others can understand and follow.

Step 5: Put a Strategy in Place. Putting a strategy in place begins by knowing why an organization exists and what its mission is. The individuals who are part of any organization need to know their roles and how they contribute to its overall success. As things change, a vision must be created to help the organization know the direction it should take. Strategy identifies the goals and ways to achieve them. Without having a strategy in place, an organization risks taking a "ready, fire, aim" mentality. Having shared values helps keep a team focused.

Step 6: Win Support. The reputation and credibility of those trying to make change happen are key to having others support their change efforts. Credibility is built over time. Individuals want to know that those they support will not hurt them and in fact will make things better for them. Understanding who your supporters are and what they can bring helps determine how much of the change strategy can be *tell* versus *sell*. Enemies can hurt. Knowing why they oppose the change effort can help in convincing them to be part of supporting it. Knowing how to influence those who are undecided can make a difference in the level of success and how quickly it is achieved. A stakeholder analysis helps identify who will need to be influenced and gives the how and why.

Step 7: Communicate Effectively. Having an effective communication process moves a change initiative from idea to action. It allows the members of a team to work together to get things done. It allows the team to communicate with stakeholders to get the information they need and to share the status of change. That way everyone knows what works and what is not working. It helps get buy-in along the way and identifies concerns stakeholders have. An effective communication strategy addresses who needs what, how, and when. It sets the tone for the work environment and affects the organization's culture.

Step 8: Overcome Challenges. Any change initiative will find those who are reluctant or opposed to the change. Changes can impact an individual's status, level of power, and ability to have an impact on the future. Knowing how to identify challenges that are both in the open and hidden is a skill that will directly affect how the change initiative progresses. Knowing when to confront directly and when to build alliances with other stakeholders will make a difference in the level of resistance you face.

Step 9: Measure Success. Change will happen. The level of success will depend on a number of factors and how well the change leaders pull resources together. An ongoing process should include a way to measure incremental changes and the level of success to the overall goals that were established in setting the strategy. Learning and being able to adjust along the way will make a difference in how successful the organization and the individuals in it are. The lessons learned will help in the ongoing process of measuring success and determining how and where resources should be allocated.

Step 10: Review Lessons Learned. Being able to learn from a current change initiative makes future change initiatives easier to undertake. Having a defined and disciplined approach for capturing what worked and what did not work, along with suggestions for how things could be better, creates a culture of constant improvement where change is not feared but looked to for the opportunities it can bring.

This book was written to be a practical resource. It is a tool you can use to understand, evaluate, and apply to make change happen. It is based on experiences and not just theory. The stories are true (but in many cases the names of individuals and organizations have been changed to fend off lawsuits before they start). Keep it handy, and put it to use.

Understand Change

If you're in a bad situation, don't worry it'll change. If you're in a good situation, don't worry it'll change.

—John A. Simone Sr.

Change has happened since the beginning of time. We are affected by it every day. Whether we choose to change or are forced to change out of necessity, it happens. Whether in the organizations we work in, the schools we attend, or the neighborhoods we live in, change is all around us. Being aware of how change works and what we can do to make a difference directly affects our lives and the level of success we achieve.

Change may come as a response to outside forces or situations. In this case, we react to change. Reactive change is change we may not want to undertake but feel we must. Change we initiate in anticipation of future opportunities or threats is proactive change. For example, were you one of the first in your field to get a cell phone, or did you wait until you were expected to have one to function? If you fit the first category, you probably looked for ways to leverage the cell phone to be more productive or effective. You took a proactive approach. If you were driven to change by the pressures around you, you experienced reactive change.

The main thing to remember is that change will happen. It can be forced on us or initiated by us, but either way we need to be prepared to deal with the change that is coming. How we respond—by choosing to be proactive or reactive—is key.

Change comes in many forms, be it political, economic, social, technological, environmental, legal, or global. There are even factors that drive change that we may not anticipate. Look at Facebook and YouTube and their impact on individuals and organizations and the way they function. While each form brings unique challenges and opportunities, all change contains similar core elements. Some changes will have a long-term impact; others will only be part of a larger ongoing cycle.

Change often creates a domino effect. One example involves the cell phone. An obvious change is that it provides greater opportunities to communicate; however, secondary changes may include increased car accidents as a result of cell phone use while driving. This leads to another change—the need for hands-free headsets—which consequently leads to more change: laws that prohibit driving and talking on a cell phone without a hands-free device. You can see the domino effect one change can have on other areas. Some changes are proactive and innovative, like the hands-free headset. Others are reactive, like the change in laws regarding cell phone use when driving.

In your role as a change leader, you can take some definite actions to help you successfully manage change. By following the 10 steps identified in this book, you will be more effective in understanding how to approach change, how to work with others, and how to accomplish more in less time.

What Is Change?

While the word *change* has numerous definitions, we are interested in change that makes something different—the act of transformation. The meaning of change will vary depending on how individuals view the change that is happening. Some will be excited and see it as an opportunity. Others will be depressed and view it as a threat.

When change happens, there are several things to keep in mind:

◆ Flexibility is key. A new way of operating will result, but in the process, trial and error may take place until the new way of operating is established. What an organization or individual does will be different from before. Some individuals may feel the need to become more connected as things change. They may look to others and try to figure out their role and how they fit in the new organizational model. The attitude is "we're in this together." For team members, this can bring an opportunity to bond by facing the challenges of change together.

◆ People will look out for themselves. Individuals often see change as a zero-sum game, with winners and losers. They look to position themselves in key areas at the expense of others. They may not know if things will be better or worse, but they want to make sure they get the best they can for themselves. Here the attitude is "I'm going to take care of myself, and I don't care about others. Only the strong survive." To overcome this, individuals need to unite as a team to help each other succeed.

◆ Sharing helps build relationships. The challenge of getting individuals to share a sense of change and what it means can often be difficult. The goal is not to defend or sell the change, but to be open to the risks and rewards of the change. Leaders who do this are the most respected and enjoy the greatest likelihood that others will listen to them. They open up to inform others of all potential results of the change—the positive, the negative, and which of these are most likely to occur.

Organizational change, or change in the workplace, affects all employees and can lead to forcing them to make adjustments in their business and personal lives.

Why do organizations undergo change? Often, new or evolving factors in the external environment force them to change, but some organizations take a proactive approach and try to initiate change to gain a competitive advantage. If they come up with a new discovery, product, or service, it can be in their best interest to change actively. Often, we see large organizations succeed in trying to keep the status quo, but as innovations happen, such as in technology, they eventually need to change, or they will be left behind. Whether the change involves a core component of how they do business or another factor that can affect their business practice, organizations must stay on top of changes in their environment and the potential impacts these changes will bring.

Types of Change

Change is generally looked at as being continuous or discontinuous. In continuous change (also known as continuous process improvement), the goal is to adjust systems and processes continually to fine-tune them and get the most you can out of what you currently have. For example, an auto manufacturer like Honda or Ford might adjust its production line to incorporate new features such as global positioning systems in its vehicles. This adjustment, while making the vehicles different, would not require a major change in the production process and would be relatively easy to incorporate. Individuals generally do not get upset when they have to make this type of change.

Discontinuous change (sometimes also referred to as re-engineering) involves a major change in business, processes, and people. Related to the first example, Honda or Ford might come up with a totally different type of vehicle, such as the hybrid or electric car. Here major processes would have to change, as would the way work gets done and the individuals involved in the process, who would likely be required to perform a new function or attend training and learn how to complete new tasks and follow new procedures. This type of change generally creates more emotion. Some individuals will be excited about the opportunity to try something new and different; others may be frustrated or fearful. As things change, so will individuals' standards. They may doubt their ability to do the new job as effectively as the old or to learn the new skills required as a result of training, or they may fear the change itself. Continuing with our earlier example, if the hybrid or electric car fails, will individuals be out of work?

This book deals mostly with discontinuous change, where a project team is brought together to make change happen, but certain methods discussed apply to both types of change.

Your Role as a Change Leader

Successful change does not just happen. It takes someone to guide the process, use the tools available, and lead the people involved. You will be looked to for direction and guidance. It is important to know and understand the overall goal of the change initiative. You will need to provide the vision, build and implement the strategy, and motivate others to perform the tasks and carry out the change. Knowing who to go to for help to get things done comes with understanding the environment and people in it.

Change leaders have personal characteristics that help them work with others. They are outgoing and approachable, show a concern for others, and have an interest in going beyond the surface level of an issue. They are willing to ask why, how, and what can make things better. They are proactive and look for ways to innovate to make improvements, whether it is utilizing technology, updating processes, or ending practices that no longer make sense.

The role of the change manager is dynamic and changing. The person needs to be flexible and know that there is not necessarily only one right answer or one right person to get the answer from. Characteristics of successful change leaders include:

- ◆ **Insight**—Know today's competitive environment, and understand that things can change to be more successful and make a difference.

- **Vision**—See the potential and the future end results that change can bring.
- **Willingness to challenge**—Look at ways to change—and in some cases challenge—existing practices and processes while being respectful and honoring the past, and drive to do what's necessary to create a successful future.
- **Ability to inspire**—Help individuals see the benefit of change, as well as understand the vision and what it means to them, to generate support for the change. It's essential to show others what success and its accompanying rewards (and the consequences of failure) look like, ideally moving people to want to take action.
- **Resourcefulness**—Have the tools and resources in place, a network that can get things done, and the ability to provide others with access to ways and resources to make things happen.
- **Ability to lead by example**—Model for others what you want them to be and do. Too often leaders fail by saying one thing and doing another. With the capability of today's media and technology, there is no way to hide. Live and do in ways you would like others to.
- **Effective communication**—Regularly communicate to various stakeholders. This is more complicated in our Web 2.0 world with a variety of media at our disposal. An effective leader feels comfortable communicating through any medium and will constantly encourage others, listen to their feedback, and make changes as needed.
- **Rewarding others**—Acknowledge good work. That gets results in the right way, whether in terms of money or praise. Too often leaders withhold praise due to ignorance or fear that individuals will want something more. The point is that if rewards and recognition are withheld, eventually an individual's efforts will be shifted in another direction. Keep in mind that others are watching. If they see certain behaviors rewarded, they will likely adopt those behaviors as well. A lack of rewards results in

individuals only looking out for themselves and not being willing to go beyond the minimum. No teamwork, collaboration, or innovation will take place. Also remember to address and correct inappropriate work and behaviors. Failure to do so sends a message that these behaviors are acceptable, and this can lead to problems that eventually must be addressed.

Stages of Change

Some changes come quickly and are open and obvious. Others take a long time to develop and occur. The key is to be prepared for how best to confront and take advantage of change when it happens. Being reactive or proactive also plays a large part in preparing for change, and as you will see in more detail in Step 4, prechange, change, and postchange are three stages individuals go through whether they choose to be reactive or proactive in their approach.

Reactive Change

Reactive change is composed of three basic stages (see Figure 1.1). The first has to do with the surprise or shock that change may induce. The second stage involves the human reaction and resistance to change. The third stage occurs when individuals realize that change is going to happen and begin to decide if they will participate in the change effort and, if so, what their roles will be. An important factor to note is that forcing individuals into a number of change scenarios on a repeated basis causes their overall level of acceptance to lessen, further disengaging them and decreasing the energy level behind their actions to initiate change. An attitude of "this too shall pass" often becomes ingrained in the culture of the organization; individuals learn to say the right thing but never actually do anything. Individuals in this environment even use phrases like "keep

FIGURE 1.1

STEP 1

The Three Basic Stages of Reactive Change

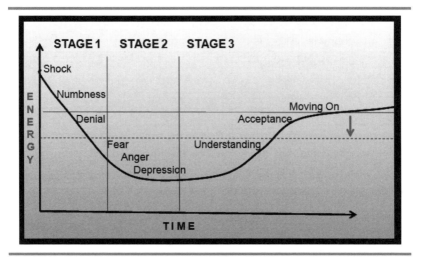

your head low," "make yourself invisible," and "just say yes," and then nothing ever happens. Be aware of this possibility and take note of signs that indicate this type of attitude exists.

Proactive Change

When change is proactive, three stages still occur, but each is very different (see Figure 1.2). The first has to do with the level of excitement that results from doing something new and different, as well as the learning and opportunities that go with it. The second stage involves the challenges of getting something done and the satisfaction that comes with accomplishment. The third stage is the realization that the individual and team have made change happen. They start to see the results of their actions. An organization that continually and effectively makes change happen sees the energy level of individuals increase. They know they can accomplish change, and they know how to make it happen. If the culture of an organization supports change, individuals will look forward to engaging in future opportunities for change.

FIGURE 1.2

The Three Basic Stages of Proactive Change

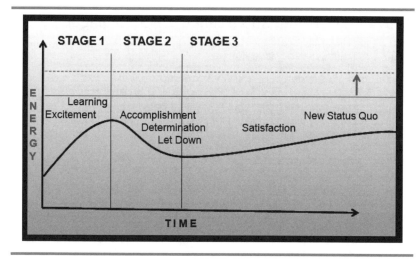

Keys to Successfully Managing Change
=====================================

The role of the change leader and the change agent team and their collective skills can make a big difference in the extent of an organization's success at managing change (see Step 3). Identifying and clearly communicating the reason and importance for change and related goals are key to achieving success. Building a strategy and getting people on board helps guide the process. Attempting to initiate change without having a strategy leads to confusion. Ask for input from key stakeholders. Making them part of the process from the beginning increases the likelihood they will accept and support it. When issues arise, you can come up with options to address them. Hiding information or giving misinformation causes individuals to fill in the blanks with information that may be worse than the truth. It also leads to credibility issues. Once credibility and consequently trust are lost, it is difficult to get them back. Break down the project into manageable steps and tasks. Set time lines and milestones to measure the change process. Acknowledge and celebrate milestones and accomplishments. Reward individuals for behavior in support of the change. Address issues from those who do not support the change or are sitting on the sidelines.

Table 1.1 lists some specific actions for change leaders to take.

TABLE 1.1

Active Roles of the Successful Change Manager

Action	Details
Build the guiding team	Get people involved with commitment and the right set of skills to accomplish the change goals.
Get the vision right	Get the team to establish a simple vision for change and a strategy to accomplish the change goals.
Develop a sense of urgency	Get people to understand they need to do something, the importance of it, and potential rewards and consequences.
Communicate regularly	Involve those who will make change happen and those who will be affected by the change that happens. Appeal to people's needs. The team needs to know the what, why, and how. Involve stakeholders to get buy-in along the way.
Empower the change team	Give people the tools and access to the resources to help make the change happen. Remove obstacles, and reward achievement.
Create short-term wins	Break the change into manageable pieces. Identify what needs to be done sequentially and what can be done in conjunction with other tasks. Share the details of the project plan.
Encourage resilience	Encourage determination. Highlight milestones. Support individuals in times of challenge. Seek additional tools and resources to help them.
Make change part of the organization's culture	Reinforce the value of successful change. Make change part of the culture. Share the lessons learned throughout the organization.

Elements of a Successful Change Initiative

No matter what type of change is being undertaken and regardless of the organization's size, certain elements make a change initiative successful.

A Clear Understanding of the Need for Change

When we look at organizations, they generally change in one of two ways: reactive or proactive. It is often easier to analyze change and its level of success after the fact. Unfortunately, analysis after the fact comes too late to make a difference today. The process often involves confusion and uncertainty as to whether a particular change is appropriate and being carried out correctly. Starting with a clear understanding of the issues and opportunities is essential in order to get change initiative off to the right start. Not understanding why will produce only activity, not productivity.

A Clear Set of Goals

Some individuals will resist change at all costs, but the majority will be open to it and may even help to make the change if they understand its purpose and potential impacts. Anyone who has been involved in a major organizational change effort such as a merger or an acquisition has seen the paralysis and lack of productivity that sets in (often for extended periods) while individuals wonder and wait to find out how the change will affect them. Open communication makes a difference. Organization leaders supported by change leaders must communicate the end goal and how to achieve it. Individuals who will be affected need an idea of how, why, and when.

An Explanation of the Risks and Rewards

Along with stating the goals and the extent to which the process for achievement has been developed, explain the potential risks and rewards. The many examples of this include the state of the automotive industry and the experiences of General Motors, Chrysler, and Ford. Don't avoid or delay sharing information on the best that can happen, the worst that can happen, and the most likely to happen.

Ongoing Communication

Regular sharing of information is important. If individuals receive no information, they make it up, and usually it is incorrect. If you don't fill in the blanks, others will, and it may be with the wrong answers. Organizational leadership must be willing to accept and answer questions that are asked. With technology, information can be checked, cross-checked, and disseminated widely and quickly. Leaders in this day and age can no longer lie or mislead. The relationships, even of those close to the individual, may never be the same.

Credibility is important; without it your influence will go nowhere. Individuals will not blindly follow, and they may oppose you simply because you did not tell them everything correctly, or lied. Share what you can. Have a good reason for what you can't.

Sharing Results on an Ongoing Basis

People want to know where they stand and how the changes around them will affect their lives. Individuals vary in their level of "need to know," but even if it's at a minimum, most people like to be informed. As you build your communication strategy, keep in mind not only what you can share, but how best you can share it. It must be ongoing; even a weekly report to state that not much has changed is better than no report at all. Are there areas not directly related to the change topic but of interest to the population? That is something you can provide. The following example is a stretch, but if you were an employee, how would such disclosure influence your perspective of the company's change effort and the leadership driving it?

> *Publish the purchase and sale data of stocks by key company executives. Most people will see purchases as a vote of support. If sales occur with a legitimate reason, say so. Before you are quick to reject this, remember publicly held companies must provide this data, which is available in the public domain, and in this day and age your employees are probably finding it anyway. End speculation before it begins.*

Related to these elements of a successful change initiative are some of the often-cited reasons that change initiatives fail. These include:

- lacking leadership that visibly supports the initiative
- communicating an unclear vision of the future
- allowing individuals to believe change is an option, not a requirement
- focusing on accomplishing tasks rather than achieving goals
- lacking a process to hear the concerns of those needed to initiate change
- failing to celebrate/reward early successes
- lacking clearly defined roles and responsibilities.

Keep these pitfalls in mind as you build your plan and strategy for change.

Onward!

Key Points to Keep in Mind

Change happens in a number of ways. Some questions to keep in mind include the following:

- What are the reasons behind the change initiative?
- How does it impact what you are doing today?
- What alternatives exist, and what are the opportunities and consequences that go with them?
- Are the goals of the change initiative clearly defined?
- Do individuals understand their roles and the risks and rewards that go with change?
- Have you identified what it's going to take from you as a change leader to help others get through it?
- From a communication perspective, what is it going to take to get buy-in and keep others informed?

WORKSHEET 1.1

Understand Why Change Happens

What's going on around you and your organization, and how is it impacting what you do?

Fill in the blank with the word *customers* and then repeat the process with other areas that may impact who you are and what you do. Examples may include *competitors, business partner relationships, uses of technology, government rules and regulations, financing options,* and *global factors.*

How are _____ changing?

What is the impact on you?

What can you do?

Do you see any patterns or trends? What are they?

How critical is it you respond to them? What happens if you do nothing?

Assess the Impact of Change

There is nothing wrong with change, if it is in the right direction.
　　　　　　　　　—Winston Churchill

Assessing the impact of an organizational change helps identify available opportunities and existing threats. By assessing the impact of change, organizations can set priorities for what to address. The assessment process gives an idea of an organization's preparedness for dealing with change and of the odds for success. Knowing how to analyze the impact of change allows the organization to best distribute and utilize its resources.

Though it can be difficult, assessing the impact of change is important because it makes a difference in how the change is viewed and addressed. An organization may take a proactive approach to change and look for ways to improve, or it may need to change because its way of functioning has been threatened by external changes. It is important to know what is changing as well as why and how. Some organizational factors to consider include customer needs, competition, finances, the state of the economy, technology, and internal capabilities. Table 2.1 illustrates these environmental factors, possible reasons for change related to each factor, and ways in which the organization can respond.

TABLE 2.1

Environmental Factors, Reasons for Change, and Potential Responses

What Is Changing?	Why? What Is Driving the Change?	Potential Response
Customer needs	Change in fashion	Decide whether to respond and, if so, how to stay on top of current and future fashions.
Competition	Desired increase in market share	Determine if competitors' markets are the same. If so, ask customers what they prefer and why. Follow up with a change strategy to better address customer needs. Keep in mind that an increase in market share does not necessarily equate to an increase in profitability.
Finances	Lower interest rates allowing borrowing at lower rates	Determine whether the lower rates allow for addressing a planned expansion.
Economy	More unemployment causing consumers to buy less	Determine whether production should be cut back.
Technology	Automation allowing better and faster customer care	Determine how much customers value the capability technology offers. Is it worth the cost?
Internal capabilities	Improved processes allowing for quicker production	Determine how one area fits in with the improvements in the other areas, based on analysis. Change as needed.

What Is Driving Your Change?

Often, organizations jump into a change effort without fully understanding why or the end goal. The first question to ask is, "Why are we making a change? Is it in response to something going on around us, or are we looking to come up with something new and better before someone else does?" If you are reacting to things going on around you, such as competitors becoming more aggressive, you need to assess the impact of their practices on how you currently operate, what your options are, and what action to take. In reacting to changes occurring around you, some questions to ask include the following:

- What change has happened that affects what we do?
- How does that change affect us and our competitive position?
- What is the level of impact: critical, serious, partial, minor, or none?
- Based on the level of impact, what do we need to look at (for example, customer relationships, core business processes, product/service mix)?
- What are our options?
- Looking at our options from the perspective of time, cost, and level of difficulty to accomplish, what action makes the most sense to take?

If your organization intends to come up with something new and better, taking a proactive approach, it needs to look at not only the competitive marketplace but also its internal capability to make change happen. In taking a proactive approach to change, some questions to ask are the following:

- What opportunities exist to make things better?
- What is the value of each opportunity?
- What resources (internal) do we have that can help us take advantage of the opportunities?
- What other resources (external) do we need that we do not have access to?
- How difficult would each of the opportunities be to accomplish?
- Based on our analysis, how are the opportunities prioritized?

Fixing Symptoms or Solving Problems

In making change happen, it is important to know what problems exist and how to address them. Unfortunately, often individuals identify and focus on addressing symptoms rather than on getting to the root cause of the problem. This happens for a number of reasons: symptoms are easy to identify, they generally don't take much effort to fix, and it is easy to show the symptom has been taken care of.

The issue with fixing a symptom is that it is temporary, like taking aspirin for chest pain. A person may temporarily feel better, but he or she may really need treatment for a more serious heart condition. The consequences of just treating the symptom could be fatal. To address this, try the "Root Cause Analysis" approach:

1. Identify the problem—The example we will use as the problem is that a major city is plagued by an increasing crime rate. Robbery and theft in particular are increasing.

2. Determine how you would address this problem—Hire more police [potential answer].

3. Ask if this is the solution to the root cause of the problem—If the city hires more police, will it slow down the increasing crime rate? Maybe, but reconsider the problem for underlying issues. Asking why robbery and theft are increasing uncovers that young people hang out on the streets at night with nothing to do.

4. Determine how you would address this problem—Set a curfew [potential answer].

5. Ask if this is the solution to the root cause of the problem—If the city enforces a curfew, will it slow down the increasing crime rate? Maybe, but reconsider the problem for underlying issues. Asking why robbery and theft are increasing and, additionally, why young people are out on the streets at night, further uncovers that young people cannot find jobs; therefore, they are out on the streets at night, and they rob and steal to get money.

6. Determine how you would address this problem—Help young people find jobs [potential answer].

7. Ask if this is the solution to the root cause of the problem—If the city helps young people find jobs, will it slow down the increasing crime rate? It's possible.

Continue this process until you find the root cause of your problem. In this case, implementing the first answer ("Hire more police") would have addressed a symptom. The third answer ("Help young people find jobs") would have shown you that jobs, not necessarily more police, are the solution. Another way to look at this issue is presented in Table 2.2.

Asking questions related to certain areas can help determine the specific impact they have on the root cause of your problem. How does each of the following—money, people, process, technology, knowledge, competition, or laws—affect your problem? Some questions to ask in seeking ways to address the problem include:

◆ Whose help or support do we need?
◆ What would it take to get the commitment of those needed to support us in solving the problem?
◆ If we fixed the identified problem, could there still be issues? What would they be? Whom would they affect?

TABLE 2.2

Root Cause Analysis

	Issue	Potential Solution	Symptom or Root Cause of the Problem
	Crime is too high.	Hire more police.	Crime is a symptom of an underlying issue.
Why?	Companies are leaving, and because people have no jobs and cannot feed their families, they steal.	Market the low cost of existing space from the businesses that left.	The fact that companies are leaving is a symptom of an underlying issue.
Why?	Companies are leaving because taxes are too high.	Find a way to lower taxes or offer a financial incentive.	"Taxes are too high" is the root cause of the problem.

Repeat this process until the lowest addressable level has been identified and addressed. From there, make an evaluation as to the cost/benefit trade-off.

Once you have identified the root cause of a problem and the areas affecting it, the next step is to determine what it relates to: skills of individuals, a lack of funding, technology, processes, or something else. Change involving each of these can have a different cost and time frame. For example, if the root cause of a problem is a lack of trained personnel working on a project, adding more people to the change initiative will only create more untrained individuals whose necessary training may take even more time away from getting the job done. See Table 2.3 for internal factors that could affect your position and possible actions to take.

TABLE 2.3

Internal Factors and Possible Actions to Take

Factor Behind the Problem and Root Cause	Possible Action and Factors to Consider
Lack of skills in our people	Training: time frame necessary to train
Lack of manpower/staff	Hire: time and cost to hire
Lack of or incorrect technology	Purchase technology: cost, time to get funding, time to get in place, time to train individuals to use
Lack of quality	Improve our quality and processes: must determine the cause of poor quality before it can be fixed
Lack of money	Find funding: evaluate possibilities and sources for funding not currently being utilized

It may come down to deciding how your strategy (see Step 5) positions your organization and what changes you need to make. For example, is your organization known for being the low-cost provider, providing the highest level of customer service, or being the most innovative organization in the field? Given external changes, how does your organization internally need to change its people, processes, and technology?

Identifying the Type of Change

The type of change your organization is going through will set the direction for the talents and skills necessary for members. As explained in Step 1, change can be seen as continuous (incremental) or discontinuous (transformational). One way to look at the context is to ask questions related to the change and use the information retrieved to categorize the type of change faced by your organization.

Questions to ask in identifying the type of organizational change include the following:

- Is the change organization-wide or within a subset of the organization?
- Is the change incremental or transformational?
- Does a plan for change exist or need to be developed?
- Has your organization been through anything like this before, and if so, what did you learn?

Answering questions related to the type of change helps classify the change and the patterns that the change may follow. It also allows for planning and building an appropriate change approach.

The environment in which your organization operates should also be analyzed. An organization's environment can be driven by any of the following:

- **Competition**—How many competitors are there? How strong are they compared to your organization? In the minds of the consumers, how does their position compare to yours? How well are they positioned? Will it be easy to get customers to switch from competitors' products and services to yours?
- **Innovation**—Is the environment one where things constantly change, such as the software or computer industry, or is it more stagnant, as with the utility industry?

- **Market characteristics**—How narrowly defined is the market you are in or work with? Are there many things to look at or only a few? How do you prioritize them?
- **Customer expectations**—How important are you to the customers you serve in your market? Are you a key part of their operation—meaning without you, they would no longer exist—or are you easily replaceable? What are the alternatives for the products and services you provide, and how easy are they to find?
- **Business partners**—To what extent do you depend on others to provide your products and services? What would happen if they went away?

In the end, it is important to understand your operating environment. If additional costs due to rules and regulations are incurred, make sure you incorporate them into your change plans.

Assessing the Impact of Change

Understanding the impact a change will have on your organization will help determine its level of importance and help you prioritize what resources (money, people, and time) must be engaged to deal with or take advantage of it. What will the change do for your organization? Will the change drive growth and help it increase in size, gain market share, or increase profitability? If your organization chooses not to change, will the impact put it out of business, cost it market share, or simply eliminate a minor part of the business?

If you are leading the change initiative, you have not only the change issues to deal with but also the people issues. You need to get people to understand and see the vision for change and what it will bring. You need to let them know how you are counting on them and what is in it for them. If individuals in the organization feel they are doing well and they are happy with the status quo, you need to show them why their current practices will no longer work. Addressing the changes around them—in regard to innovation, changing customer needs and wants, and competitor moves—can help get their attention and commitment.

Here is an example demonstrating the importance of adaptability and the effects of change.

Less than 20 years ago, Blockbuster video stores were opening on every other corner. Customers loved the concept. They could go into a local retail location, pick out one of the newest video releases at a reasonable cost, and take it home to watch in comfort. Investors drove the stock price up, customer segments grew, and employees had great benefits and what they thought were long-term, secure jobs. There was no reason to look at changing. Then along came changes in technology (DVDs) and innovations (mailing capability), both of which allowed a company called Netflix to come up with a more cost-effective business model. Customers liked what they saw, and their loyalty shifted. They no longer had to go to the store and worry about a video being out of stock. This convenience, along with more flexible return terms, allowed Netflix to capture a significant amount of Blockbuster's business. In a short amount of time, Blockbuster's once great business model was no longer relevant. Stuck in its ways, the company eventually declared bankruptcy. But again, it's important to remember that change always continues. Netflix needs to be able to deal with changes in technology, which now allows customers to immediately download videos without having to wait. The point is that you have to continuously monitor your environment and be open to change. Examples like this can help you, as the change manager, convince individuals of the need for openness and change.

Getting individuals to understand the motivation for change is one thing. Actually affecting them directly is another. A great feeling arises when an organization is growing; current employees have new opportunities, and new employees are needed. In other cases, change will bring a reduction in human resources. Individuals will be anxious and wonder who will be cut. Often those who remain have "survivor's syndrome" and become unproductive, wondering if they will be the next to go. The culture of the organization deteriorates, and individuals become unmotivated. The best way to deal with the uncertainty that comes with change is to communicate. You may not have all the answers, but being open and treating people fairly gives you credibility. Set a regular time for communication— on a weekly basis or even more frequently; even if there is nothing new to share, it shows your openness. Open communication also gives individuals a chance to provide you with information and feedback you can use to help others. Being fair is key.

I personally have been with organizations that have handled reductions in force well and those that have not. It does make a difference. If an organization takes the time to communicate with individuals and help them move on (for example, by providing job leads, networking, and even separation funds), individuals tend to remember and help, or at least not hurt, their former organization. Organizations that call people in, tell them it is their last day, and immediately escort them out the door tend to set a tone of rejection and animosity. Chances for any future support are slim, and considering the ability to communicate quickly through technology and the Internet, word can quickly get out and negativity can spread.

If the change occurs in response to environmental factors (competition, technology, laws, customer preferences, and so on), the best approach is based on understanding the factors and being able to respond to and overcome them. If the change is self-based, originating with the goal of changing the environment, the approach allows for taking a lead and working through various scenarios involving the change and the industry in which the organization operates.

How will making or not making a change affect your organization? Will changing make it more successful? With the number and various types of changes, organizations need to be able to effectively assess the potential impact of changes they make and of those made by others around them. Some changes—for example, implementing a wireless network in an office—can save on costs and will have only a minor impact on productivity, while a change in laws, such as limiting acceptable accounting practices, can put an organization out of business if it is not prepared for the repercussions.

To assess the potential impact of a change, look at these factors:

◆ What is behind the change? Is your organization driving the change, or is change being forced upon it? How much control does your organization have over this change?

◆ Evaluate the best- and worst-case scenarios. What will happen if your organization does nothing? What will happen if your organization attempts the change and fails? What will happen if your organization succeeds in changing?

◆ How well prepared is your organization to undertake the change? Can the change be implemented without a problem, or will your organization be stretched to take it on? Where can other resources be found, if needed, and at what cost?

◆ What are your organization's competitors doing? Are they making or being affected by the same change? Is something being forced on the industry (for example, government regulations) that competitors can partner with your organization to combat?

◆ How will the change affect your organization's business practices and profitability? Does the cost of change outweigh the benefit?

Assessing the Organization's Readiness for Change

Realizing the need for change and wanting to change in order to take advantage of an opportunity, or being forced to change due to threats and potential consequences, is just the beginning. The next step involves evaluating your organization's ability—and its members' desire—to take on the change initiative.

From an organization perspective, as the change leader, you need to look at resources:

- What funds are available to support the change?
- Which members of your organization can be part of the change team and help others through the change process?
- How will working on the change initiative affect existing day-to-day functions?
- What internal resources (technology, equipment, supplies) are available to use? Will your organization have to find resources? Identify who will approve and allocate.
- Will external resources be needed? How reliable are they?

The most important factor in assessing readiness for change is often the individuals in your organization and their motivation for making change happen. Going through their minds will be the following questions:

- What does this change mean for me?
- Is it the right thing to do?
- Will I feel good about doing it?
- What if I don't do it?

Their thinking will show up in behaviors. Individuals will be asking questions, questioning proposed changes, talking to others to get their opinions, and eventually taking a stand to support or resist the change effort.

Understanding how individuals assess the change facing them helps an organization and its leadership understand the hopes, concerns, and fears of its members. Being able to address and respond to issues and foresee potential issues before they become major obstacles allows an organization to address individuals' concerns and increase their readiness for change.

Stages in Assessing Readiness

1. **Monitoring**—Readiness for change starts by monitoring the environment, or looking for opportunities and threats that can affect how your organization functions. Looking

externally for opportunities and having an idea of what internal areas could affect your organization allows for monitoring and evaluating potential changes. Looking at what interests and concerns your organization on a regular basis helps ensure it is not caught off guard by changes around it that can affect how it does business.

2. **Assessing**—After identifying potential impacts, your organization needs to gather data about *how* it may be affected. Whether it is the rate of inflation in the overall economy or the price competitors charge for their products and services, which directly affects what and how much they buy, it is important to continuously monitor data that can have an impact. The data can be gathered in a number of ways, some directly from those involved or through third parties such as industry organizations. The data will help project what changes or adjustments your organization may want to make in the future.

3. **Analyzing**—Along with gathering data, you need the ability to analyze and understand its potential impacts. Both quantitative and qualitative data can be analyzed. Looking at numbers such as revenue, cost of production, and profit helps from a quantitative perspective. Conversations with customers related to satisfaction and future needs can produce qualitative data, which helps organizations understand potential issues and opportunities that go beyond the numbers. Compare these numbers to current industry standards or to historical data to see what changes have happened over time. The goal is to be able to understand what the data means and how to analyze it to determine the best changes for your organization.

4. **Action**—Based on the analysis of data, your organization needs to decide what to do going forward. This is an important point because organizations often have the data and information in front of them but fail to act until it is too late. The best decisions are made based on what a change manager knows. You may have heard

the term *paralysis by analysis*, which happens when organizations continually look at and analyze data but never do anything with it. The point is that organizations need to make decisions and take action as part of the change process. This is where change leaders can make a difference. It takes initiative to get things done.

Taking action once a decision is made involves lining up support from those who can affect how the organization changes. Lining up the resources and ensuring commitment is the first step in taking action to make change happen. Involving those who support the organization on a regular basis helps keep the momentum going.

Key Points to Keep in Mind

Being able to assess the impact of change helps guide what should be done to make it happen. You should:

- ◆ Know what is driving the change.
- ◆ Make sure you address the root cause of the problem, not just the symptoms.
- ◆ Know what factors are behind the change and identify ways to deal with each factor.
- ◆ Understand the readiness of the organization to deal with the change so you know what level of selling needs to be done to get individuals onboard.
- ◆ Know the stages of change and what should be addressed in each phase.
- ◆ Know what action to take, get ready to take action, and take action.

WORKSHEET 2.1

Assess the Impact of Change

Change is always happening. The key is what it means to you and your organization.

Think through some of the changes going on around you. What would happen if you did nothing, tried to do the same thing as others in your situation, or tried something totally new and different? Consider each change with each of the following questions and see what comes to mind.

What is changing around you?

What if you did nothing in response to this change?

What if you tried to do what everyone else in the same situation is trying to do?

What if you tried something different? What would it be? What are the potential risks and rewards?

N O T E S

Assemble a Change Management Team

OVERVIEW

Who needs to be on the team?

Skills needed on the team

Working cross-functionally

Assessing individuals

Setting the agenda

Key points to keep in mind

Sow a thought, and you reap an act;

Sow an act, and you reap a habit;

Sow a habit, and you reap a character;

Sow a character, and you reap a destiny.

—Charles Reade

As mentioned in Step 1, change is inevitable. What makes a difference is how individuals and organizations respond to the change event. Successful change initiatives start with a detailed analysis of the situation and the accompanying threats and opportunities; they include a vision of the change's meaning for the organization as well as a strategy and plan to carry out the change. Still, an even more crucial element is having a team in place to execute those items. Who you choose to join the change management team and how the team members work together will often determine the extent to which your change initiative achieves success.

Who Needs to Be on the Team?

Usually an executive in the organization, a key customer, a business partner, or a member of the board of directors comes up with an idea for how an organization can change to be more successful or how it needs to change to survive. As momentum builds, a department or an individual is identified to conduct a feasibility study to see if the project makes sense. If the project is determined to be viable, a project manager, often someone who was involved in the feasibility study, is assigned. An executive sponsor is also generally assigned to the initiative to oversee the project from a high level and monitor its progress. Along with this, the executive sponsor is involved in acquiring more resources and funding for the project.

Once the change initiative has been identified, a team needs to be brought together, with the right number of people with the right skills. Often, organizations start with lean teams and, when things go wrong, throw more bodies on the project in an effort to catch up. The projects often fall further behind because the existing team members need to take time to acquaint and train the new members.

In putting a change team together, follow these steps:
1. Review the change vision and the goals your organization needs to accomplish as a result.
2. Based on the goals identified, determine what tasks your organization needs to accomplish in order to achieve each of the goals. Some overlap may occur, but it is best to identify each specific goal, which will give you a way to measure progress. This list of tasks will serve as a guide for team members and as a tool to show the project sponsor and stakeholders the degree of progress toward accomplishing the goals.
3. Look at the tasks that your organization needs to accomplish and see how they fit together. For example, can they be categorized into tasks related to finance, marketing, engineering, information technology, manufacturing, or other specific areas?
4. Meet with leaders from the functional task areas identified above and get input on the level of manpower needed

to accomplish the identified tasks in the available time frame. This is also a good point for a reality check to see if leaders in these specific areas feel you have everything covered and if all tasks have been identified that need to be accomplished to achieve the change goals. Note that organizations sometimes work with external consultants who have expertise in these areas, as well as models and guidelines they apply to breaking down the project goals into tasks and necessary levels of manpower to achieve the goals within a defined period of time.

5. Based on this input, build the requirements for the number and type of individuals needed on the team. Certain projects will require a core team, whose members stay throughout the project, and a secondary team comprising other individuals with specific expertise who join and leave the team as defined by the time line and phases identified. A core team starts with a project manager, someone who may have had some involvement in the preliminary analysis to consider the change project for feasibility. From there, based on the identified tasks, your organization can create roles and identify positions for members of the team.

Usually, the core project team consists of the project manager, someone to track finances, and a liaison or liaisons to the various areas affected by the change (see Table 3.1). As the change project plan is executed, individuals with other backgrounds and skills may join and leave the team. For example, a thorough needs assessment would be conducted at the beginning of a project and require more project team members with skills in needs analysis and more time of members from the area being affected. At the end of a project, more actual day-to-day end users to test the new product, process, or technology would be needed to make sure all needs have been addressed.

Change Team Makeup

Be ...ssed	Team Member	Responsibility
Overall project management	Project Manager	Responsible for managing the overall project, executing project strategy, team member selection and support, and managing day-to-day project operations. Also responsible for the project's overall success. Needs to communicate with project sponsors on status, issues, and opportunities.
Project finances	Financial Analyst	Responsible for tracking finances, monitoring budget versus money spent, measuring project progress to spending targets, and tracking personnel, materials, and supply expenses.
Change relationships	Business Unit Liaison (More than one person may be needed to fill this role, depending on the functional business areas affected by the change.)	Responsible for managing the relationship between the business unit function being affected and providing input to the project team. Also responsible for making sure areas of change are addressed and everything that could be affected is considered. Helps coordinate the transition and migration from the old processes to the new.
Project execution (doing the actual work related to the change project)	Members of the team who will work on the actual project tasks. (The number of these team members and their background will vary depending on the project's level of difficulty and the skills needed to execute the tasks. A financial change project will require more individuals with a finance background, for example, and an information technology change will require more individuals with an IT background.)	Responsible for executing the tasks as defined in the change plan and as assigned by the project manager. Also responsible for reporting progress and addressing issues as they come up.

Skills Needed on the Team

Implementing change requires a variety of personal attributes and skills for all members of the change management team. From an attributes perspective, do individuals have

- the ability to communicate effectively?
- the ability to work with others from diverse functional groups?
- a willingness to learn and teach others?
- the ability to coach and mentor others?
- the people skills needed to make it through difficult times?
- a commitment to making the change initiative successful?
- the ability to work well with others, even under pressure?
- the ability to work with uncertainty?
- personal characteristics that lead others to respect them?
- an openness to sharing and helping others, being able to give as well as receive feedback?
- the motivation to truly be part of the change team and see the project through to a successful completion?

From a "skills to get the job done" perspective, do individuals

- have the necessary technical skills?
- know the subject matter they will be working with?
- understand the importance of the change initiative to the business units they are working with and how it affects their overall business strategy?
- understand how the change initiative will affect both the organization and its employees?
- have previous experience working on a change team and know what skills it takes to make change happen?

See Table 3.2 for a list of desirable skills and attributes essential to particular members of the core project team.

TABLE 3.2

Skills and Attributes Desired for Core Members of the Change Management Team

Role	Skills and Attributes Desired	Things to Look For
Project Manager	• Ability to manage multiple tasks • Ability to manage a group of diverse individuals • Ability to track and keep on track the change initiative • Ability to quickly build relationships with stakeholders • Ability to motivate and effectively lead a team	• Past record • Support from areas affected. Do they support the individual going into the project, and will they be consulted before the project begins? • Skills in the subject matter area to be addressed • Interpersonal skills required to work with a group in a project setting • Previous leadership roles
Financial Analyst	• Ability to track expenses to a budgeted amount • Ability to do cost forecasting • Knowledge of project financial reporting	• Previous change project work • Experience in project budgeting and forecasting • Contacts in the finance group that can help in the financial analysis area • Previous work in cost analysis finance
Business Unit Liaison	• Ability to work with others in the business units • Good working knowledge of the functional area to be worked with • Ability to take user requirements and translate them into change project tasks • Need to connect people—those who know information that can affect a project with those who need to know so they can change accordingly	• Previous change work experience • Effectiveness of existing relationships within the business units • Functional knowledge of subject areas as well as credibility in those areas • Recommendations by stakeholders
Change Team Members	• Technical skills to get the work done • People skills to get along with others on the team and in groups they need to work in • Knowledge of the organization, its processes, and its functions • Knowledge of how to get things done in the organization	• Past experience on change projects • Reputation within the organization • Motivation and interest in doing what it takes to be part of the project team • Career goals and how they fit with work of the change project

Working Cross-Functionally

A challenge with change teams and one of the reasons they often fail involves a mismatch of needs, personality conflicts, and issues that go unresolved because no one wants to make the effort to address them. Often the focus is strictly on goals and not on how they will be achieved. Individuals also tend to focus on self-interest and place it above the overall goals of the team. To address this issue, spend time up front to get each individual's perspective on the change project and his or her role therein. Having well-defined rules (team norms) can make the process of working together much easier.

Assessing Individuals

Assessing potential team members identifies the talents and resources they can bring to the change team. An assessment helps an organization identify internally available resources and those that must be sought from outside.

The assessing process can range from interviewing individuals to more formal assessments on character and personality. Table 3.3 includes areas to consider and possible questions to ask in interviewing potential team members.

Generally, individuals are assessed from two perspectives. One involves how the individual—regardless of technical skills—fits in and helps the change team work effectively. Look for an individual who not only has the skills required for his or her role, but also pitches in to make sure everyone is doing OK, whether by helping to make copies of a document for a meeting or by cleaning up the tables after the meeting. These skills are the intangibles that make other team members better and motivate them to work toward change.

The other perspective addresses the technical aspects of an individual's capabilities. The objective here is to determine the existence of one's knowledge, skills, and abilities. For example, can an accountant pass the Certified Public Accounting exam and earn the

TABLE 3.3

Interview Guidelines

Interview Area	Possible Questions
Capability (to get the job done)	Have you done work similar to what we are going to do on this project?
	Based on what you know about this project, what do you think you will need to do? Do you feel you will need any other training or support to get it done?
	Given the objectives of the change plan, do you see any issues?
Interest (of individuals in being part of the change team)	Are you interested in working on this project?
	What do you feel you can learn?
Commitment (of individuals to the team)	Can you put in the time needed to make this change initiative a success?
	Are there any events such as school, family, or other outside obligations that could affect your ability to fully commit to this project?
	This change initiative could require nontraditional work hours and practices. Can you make the commitment to do what needs to be done to make this change a success?

CPA designation? Such certifications from well-respected organizations let you know that individuals who have earned these designations have a set of skills that can be counted on.

If the individuals being considered for change team membership lack the necessary technical skills, they may be trained and brought up to speed quickly. It must be determined whether the individuals involved can learn the necessary skills in the time frame that is allowed.

An organization should have a short- and long-term career strategy for individuals to determine if they need training in certain areas—not just to get them through the change process, but for ongoing enrichment to help the organization. A decision here is often based on build or buy. Is your organization set up to help individuals grow and develop, or does it seek and acquire outside talent when needed?

Setting the Agenda

Once the change management team is built, a meeting must be set to discuss objectives. As the change project manager, you will benefit from meeting with other leaders of the organization who may be needed for support or may be affected by the change. Share what you know and listen to the opinions and concerns of others. You may also choose to keep a scorecard of the level of support such individuals may provide or the level of resistance they may put up. If possible, you should identify the reasons behind their positions.

After the initial meeting, follow-up meetings should be regularly scheduled. In early stages where there is more of a need to learn and understand what others are doing and what they need, the meetings should be more frequent. As the project goes along, weekly status meetings generally give everyone a chance to talk about

◆ tasks and accomplishments of the past week
◆ challenges or issues and ideas for addressing them
◆ plans for each individual or group for the next week.

Key Points to Keep in Mind

Assembling the right team of individuals has a direct impact on the level of success a change initiative achieves.

◆ Start with a clear understanding of the change goals.
◆ Decide, based on the goals, what tasks must be completed to accomplish them.
◆ Use tasks to define the roles of team members.
◆ Don't just accept anyone available to be on the team.
◆ Bring the right team members together; assess them for interpersonal skills as well as technical skills.
◆ Bring the team together early in the process and ensure that all members know the goals and their roles in achieving them.

WORKSHEET 3.1

Team Member Requirements: Growth Strategy Change Plan

Created: _____ Updated: _____

Purpose: The Team Member Requirements worksheet helps to identify required members based on skills needed to complete a project. Use this worksheet for the overall term of a change project or for change based on a phased project approach.

Role	Potential Individuals	Priority	Notes
Financial Manager • Track project financials. • Reconcile financials with finance department. • Track project expenses. • Monitor time and attendance.			
Marketing Representative • Bring marketing perspective. • Liaise with sales and marketing departments.			
IT Support and Development • Ensure project has technical tools. • Define change project requirements. • Liaise with IT department to ensure systems can support organizational changes.			
Manufacturing • Provide perspective of existing capability. • Identify what is needed in the changed environment.			

Build a Vision for Change

STEP **4**

Vision without action is a dream. Action without vision is simply passing the time. Action with vision is making a positive difference.
—Joel Barker

Individuals involved in a change initiative need to know why things are changing and, more importantly, what it means for them. Having a vision for change tells people where the organization is going and how they fit into it. Providing a purpose and vision of the future as a result of a change gives individuals a sense of community and belonging. It helps them feel as though their efforts are part of creating something that will make a difference.

In his 2001 book, *Good to Great*, Jim Collins looks at how good companies become great companies. Over a five-year period, his team studied 1,435 companies and found only 11 that met the criteria of moving from good to great: changing their practices to make a difference. In these cases, a vision for change led individuals to take initiative and to take the necessary steps to stand out. The companies that chose to change, and had the discipline to make the needed changes, became great. The ability of these organizations' leaders to simplify the complex world in which they operated into a single organizing principle unified, organized, and acted as a guide for all decisions the organizations had to make. Envisioning what change could bring inspired people to make a difference. Collins thus points to three elements that help drive an organization's vision for change: (1) an organization's reason for existing, its purpose or mission, which gives its members something to identify with; (2) a set of core values, which provides members with expectations for fulfilling responsibilities and guidelines for behavior; and (3) a set of goals, or, as Collins refers to them, "Big Hairy Audacious Goals" (p. 202). A change vision helps individuals understand where the organization is going and why.

A change vision comes about as a result of an organization looking for changes in its external environment and its internal capabilities (see Figure 4.1). Internally, the organization considers the strengths and weaknesses of its function, people, and process. It takes into consideration its ability to change and innovate. Externally, it looks at changing customer needs, changes in technology, and competitive positioning, considering possible opportunities and potential threats. A change vision differs from an organizational vision in that the latter is the organization's overriding vision for what it can be and what it stands for. An organization can have multiple change visions. The point is that each relates to the specific change initiative and what that initiative can do for the organization.

Why Is a Change Vision Important?

A vision for change is important because it gives an organization a sense of how it deals with surrounding changes. The reality is that organizations rarely stay the same. They either grow or die, acquire or become acquired, create and innovate or become obliterated. It is plain and simple, as history shows. Look at any 10-year period of the Fortune 500. How many currently listed companies were not there 10 years ago, how many previously listed companies have been acquired by others, and how many have fallen off the list altogether? Film worked well when you needed it for a camera,

FIGURE 4.1

Vision for Change: External and Internal Considerations

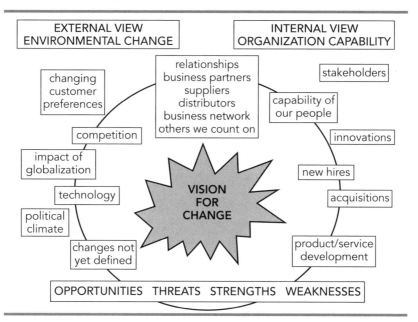

but technology changed while Kodak did not—and the company eventually declared bankruptcy in 2010. Do you remember RCA (Radio Corporation of America), once a Fortune 25 company known for its televisions, radios, and record players? The business model changed. Foreign competitors, first from Japan and now from Korea and China, have found better, faster, and cheaper ways to deliver these types of products. Speaking of record players, have you ever even seen one? Changes can make a product or service obsolete to the point where the only place you will find one is in a museum. Look at this from a growth and innovation perspective. There is Apple Computer, or is it Apple, the largest seller of music online? How about companies that have combined areas of change such as technology, global reach, and consumer tastes to create companies like Google and Facebook—and, yes, Facebook is a company with a vision. Organizations succeed because they have a vision for change and turn that vision into a reality. Having a vision for change is the start of making change happen.

Creating a Vision for Change

Taking a proactive approach to change (see Step 1) centers not only on creating a change vision, but also on communicating that vision to employees before, during, and after the change. Keep in mind these three stages—prechange, change, and postchange—when creating your vision for change.

Prechange

Before the actual work of change begins, an organization must establish the change vision. Why is the organization making a change, and what does it hope to accomplish by changing? Use this vision when meeting with the project sponsor and other stakeholders to get feedback on what is proposed. It may need to be adjusted based on the feedback you get as you go. Getting buy-in along the way helps ensure agreement later and can also inspire the various stakeholders to become active and supportive change participants. A vision for change should consider a number of factors:

- the purpose for change and goals of the organization
- measures of progress and expectations for success; indications that the organization has realized the change vision
- how the organization will operate after the change
- how the culture supports or needs to adjust to support the changed organization
- the project time frame, if applicable
- the values of the organization
- any roadblocks that could get in the way of achieving the change.

Change

During the change process, it is important to ensure that the change team is up and running as planned—that is, operating according to the change vision. The change manager must address any issues as soon as possible. Given the visibility typical of change projects, being up-front about issues is key for both team members and the change manager. Up-front communication also helps to identify individuals' true levels of commitment, as well as to make sure committed resources are available and work is going according to the vision (see Step 7 for how to communicate effectively).

When building a change vision, the change manager needs to keep in mind those individuals the change will affect and what it means to them.

Depending on the size and nature of the impending change, your organization may want to inform outside individuals about the vision for change. Some of these external people might include the following:

- ◆ **Customers**—A vision tells them that your organization is changing and describes the change process and the path to accomplishment.
- ◆ **Business partners**—A vision lets them know the unique way your organization operates and that they can count on you to continue to provide products and services throughout the change process.
- ◆ **Members of your organization**—A vision establishes new standards and sets the tone for expectations in terms of behavior.
- ◆ **Other stakeholders as identified**—A vision identifies your organization's commitment and how making changes will help you accomplish your goals.

Individuals need support in their attempts to attain the organization's vision for change.

Postchange

Following implementation of the change, it is a good idea to revisit the change vision and determine the degree of achievement. Is the change achieved the "new normal" or just a step in an ongoing change process? If the latter, the change manager might choose to further individuals' alignment with and commitment to the change vision by publicizing individual and group achievement through the recognized communication channels and modeling leadership behavior.

Either way, the change manager must answer any questions and resolve any outstanding issues, making sure everyone is on the same page as to the new way of operating. Moving forward, the change manager can keep the vision alive in actions and behaviors by documenting and sharing lessons learned and determining how past change processes can help support future change initiatives.

Additional Factors Affecting the Change Vision

Organizations spend a lot of time and energy creating mission and vision statements. The purpose of these statements is to act as concise and direct messages to let everyone, internal and external, know why the organization exists and what it is trying to accomplish. Values create the culture of an organization and determine how it functions on a day-to-day basis. They address the expected behaviors of individuals and the consequent reward or punishment.

Confusion often erupts between an organization's vision, mission, and values and their impact on changes the organization attempts. A vision for change is meant to be transformational and give a picture of the changed organization. It looks at the ideal and what the organization strives to accomplish and be known for.

In embarking on a change process, the vision for change should act as the guiding light for the organization's members, or as a way for individuals to identify with its purpose and be motivated to accomplish goals and put in their best effort to help achieve the desired change. In decision making or dealing with difficult situations, the vision for change stands out and serves as a guide. It is future oriented, looking at what can be. The intended change could be as direct as an annual increase in profits, but the inspiration is not the same.

Different from a vision for change is an organization's mission. A mission statement describes what an organization does and how it tries to accomplish things on a day-to-day basis. It tells the world what products and services the organization has to offer. In building a mission statement, an organization should look at its culture, the way individuals work with each other, and the processes involved in accomplishing goals. A mission statement should consider what the organization does from a products and services perspective: how the products are manufactured (for example, all recycled materials, safe to the environment, or made in the United States) or, if providing services, what guidelines the organization follows (for example, all calls returned within 24 hours, satisfaction guaranteed, establishing a level of ongoing support). The mission should analyze customers and potential customers and what is important to them (for example, price, quality, innovation). Laws, rules, and regulations can also impact how a mission is accomplished. Future direction, if the organization seeks to grow or develop in certain product or market areas, should also be considered. Finally, answering the question "What about this organization sets it apart from others?" should be incorporated.

Values represent an organization's culture. They set standards as far as acceptable behaviors and provide guidelines for dealing with individuals both inside and outside the organization. Values should be based on how the organization works with its customers, treats its employees, or cares for its stakeholders. Organizations usually come up with a list of (three to seven) core values for their members to live by. These values guide members' choices and actions.

For example, the U.S. Air Force follows "Integrity First, Service Before Self, and Excellence in All We Do" as its three core values. "Integrity First" sets the standard for how individuals operate with each other and the public they serve. All members receive regular reminders that being part of the organization means providing a service for others, or "Service Before Self." "Excellence in All We Do" sets the standard for all actions by the organization. All decisions and interactions are based on these core values. Note that when an individual or a group of individuals disregards the organization's basic values, the cultural standards often decline, and the focus becomes more on what individuals can get away with rather than what standards they need to live up to. Today's proactive organizations focus more on doing the right things in the right way than on the "just do it" model many lived by in the past. Some also consider their values a moral compass when ethical decisions come into play. Values can help drive a vision for change since they are the basis for the organization's existence.

A strategic plan provides the specific details on goals and the day-to-day activities required to accomplish them. It looks to the vision as the overall guide for long-term accomplishment (for example, over three to five years). It looks to the mission for day-to-day operations, letting individuals know their responsibilities and providing a time line for getting things done. It looks to the values when considering *how* to get things done. Intent, capability, and resources help formulate the strategic plan. When an organization contemplates change, a vision to help focus individuals comes into play. It sets the direction and may eventually lead to a change in the organization's mission, vision, and, in some cases, values.

Describing an organization's culture often requires descriptive terms such as *collaborative*, *strong*, *creative*, and *respectful*, but these terms don't give us much to work with. I remember working with a consulting firm on a change initiative, and one representative reminded me that his firm had a "strong culture." When I asked what that meant, the individual indicated that *everyone* believed strongly in and lived closely by the founding principles of the organization. My next question was whether he thought that belief would ease or complicate the change effort—to which I don't think I ever received an answer. Whether the culture is strong or weak is not the determining factor. What makes a difference is realizing and cooperating with the culture. A good place to start with organizational and cultural change is to obtain support and leadership from individuals who are respected and looked to for guidance within the organization. Having a vision for change keeps individuals focused on their goals and anticipated accomplishments.

On certain occasions, an organization's strong culture presents an issue. C.K. Prahalad (2010) coined the term *forgetting curve* to identify behaviors, practices, and beliefs that are no longer productive and in some cases counterproductive. Sometimes, when it comes to making change happen, accelerating the forgetting curve can be more important to organizations than accelerating the learning curve.

Key Points to Keep in Mind

A vision sets the course, and getting individuals to understand it will determine the level of buy-in you get from them. To accomplish this, it's important to do the following:

- Identify areas that can impact the change and incorporate them into building the vision for change.
- Keep the change vision simple so others can understand it.
- Don't assume individuals will automatically buy in; it takes communication to get commitment.
- Common values and interests help get buy-in.
- Get input from those who will be impacted and provide a way for individuals to give feedback.
- Address issues head on.

WORKSHEET 4.1

Building a Change Vision

Building a change vision gives individuals something to identify with. It looks at what will be different and why it matters. The goals of and reason for the change should be addressed.

Take the following steps to build a change vision:

1. Describe why the change initiative is being undertaken.

    a. Due to internal strengths or weaknesses

    b. Due to external opportunities or threats.

2. What is at risk if a change is not made?

3. How does the change vision differ from the existing corporate vision?

4. How does the change vision affect individuals and what they do today?

5. What are the rewards of making change happen?

The answers to these questions will help build the vision for change. Once the change vision is built, it should be shared throughout the organization and with key external business partners. A vision projects the future of the organization and can draw input from such partners to ensure they buy in and participate in the process.

NOTES

Put a Change Strategy in Place

What's the use of running if you are not on the right road?

—German proverb

STEP 5

Determining that an organization needs to change to be more successful is a starting point. Figuring out how to initiate that change often determines success or failure. A change strategy looks at how to make things happen with the resources available. The overall guide on what change is desired and how it will be achieved, a change strategy addresses the vision for change and what it will do for the organization; it includes the goals to accomplish, and addresses the issues that exist, the tasks involved in the initiative, and the plans for making it happen.

An organization's change strategy may be driven by

◆ changing customer preferences
◆ innovations in technology
◆ changes in how competitors do business
◆ new competitors entering the market
◆ changes in how products and services are used
◆ development of new products to meet customer needs

- changing cost structures
- changes in government regulations.

All of these influences and others that show up unexpectedly along the way will affect an organization's strategy and how it is implemented.

What Components Make Up a Change Strategy?

They say the shortest distance between two points is a straight line. If only it were that easy to build a change strategy. The challenges in keeping day-to-day operations running while taking on a change initiative can create a tough situation. Having a strategy and knowing what resources are available to support it can help minimize issues as they come up.

In some cases, the change strategy is broken down into three component areas:

1. **Strategic**—This is the overall plan as an idea, or what the organization hopes to accomplish, including end goals that will be achieved.
2. **Operational**—Identify what will be done in each area (the who and what).
3. **Tactical**—What are the specific tasks to be completed? These should include functional areas, names assigned, and deadlines to be met.

A change strategy should consider the following:
- **Your organization's current abilities (competencies)**— What do you do well and not so well?
- **The environment your organization functions in**—How do your customers, competitors, and business partners see the organization? Do individuals see it as a trusted source, or do they avoid it?
- **Alternatives**—Do competitors offer other options for products and services? Obsolescence and innovation can have a major impact on alternatives.

- **Available resources**—Are people, sources of funding, and technology on hand to help make things happen?
- **The future of your organization**—What does it mean to the stakeholders involved?
- **The end results**—What is the probability of success, and what are the implications of failure?

Being Aware of Your Boundaries

When crafting your change strategy, keep in mind that you may be limited by rules, policies, and procedures. These may be imposed internally by the organization as part of its culture and values, or externally by industry and government. Examples of external factors include safety regulations set by the Occupational Safety and Health Administration (OSHA), environmental guidelines by the Environmental Protection Agency (EPA), and financial influences (Congress, taxes, laws). Be aware of these boundaries and find ways to work within them.

Organizations must put in place accepted ways of operating based on their culture and values. Having a set of rules, policies, and procedures gives individuals guidelines for following accepted organizational practices.

Rules are the absolutes; they provide order and a way to deal with events. Violation of a rule leads to punishment. An example would be a school that has "no tolerance" for cheating on tests. Any individual caught cheating on a test is expelled. This is a set rule and cannot be overridden by a teacher or an administrator.

Policies are generally accepted ways of doing things. They give guidance but are not as rigid as rules. There is some room for interpretation and application as appropriate to the situation or task at hand. Not following a policy may be questioned, but the consequences of breaking policy are not as strict as those of violating a rule. Continuing with our previous example, the school, instead of having a strictly defined rule against cheating on a test, may have a policy. In this case, the policy may say that cheating is not allowed on tests and individuals caught doing so will be punished. It leaves the "punishment" more open-ended as to what it will entail and who will impose it. The policy also leaves discretion as to the level of cheating and the level of punishment imposed.

Procedures are the day-to-day ways that things get done. Sometimes they align closely with rules and policies, and other times they do not. The alignment (or lack thereof) tends to come from individuals seeking to accomplish a task and may evolve based on a change. A frequent explanation for not following a procedure is that the individual feels it needs improvement, and often he or she can show how. Often, this leads to things being done in a better, faster, and cheaper way, but how does it fit with the organization's established practices, and what does it mean to deviate from these practices? What are the consequences of not following a procedure? Will the individual or the procedure be reviewed, will the situation be ignored altogether, or will the individual be punished for not conforming to the generally accepted practices of the organization? Following with our previous example, it may be stated among school administrators that individuals should not cheat on tests but not that there is a penalty involved. In fact, if cheating is found, the instructor may see if it helped in the learning process for all involved and may decide that group tests would be more effective than individual tests. This instructor's procedure could then be changed from testing students individually to testing them in a group.

Rules, policies, and procedures set the tone for an organization's culture during a time of change.

Change Management Planning

The purpose of a change management plan is to coordinate changes across the entire project and for all groups and individuals. The plan helps ensure changes are agreed on, the process is understood, and goals are set in terms of deliverables, time, and cost. It is a living document that can be changed as things change in the organization's environment.

Goals of a change management plan include reaching agreement on changes to be made, how they will be evaluated and tracked, and how they will affect the overall direction of the project. The plan should describe specific tasks and who is responsible for them, available funding and how it will be used, and how success will be measured. A risk assessment is often included to show what could go wrong along with a best-case and worst-case scenario. See Table 5.1 for an example of a change management plan for a fictional corporation embarking on a mission to improve its growth strategy.

Change plans can be modified to apply to an entire organization or broken down into subparts for various divisions, groups, and teams. A plan may also vary by geographic region, product line, industry served, organizational capability, or competitive pressures the organization faces.

Once an organization has scanned its environment, the goal-setting process can begin.

STEP 5

TABLE 5.1

Change Management Plan: SunSenior Corporation

Initiative: Growth Strategy Change Plan

Project Sponsor(s) Name—Title	Background
Dr. Monica Sun—CEO	Dr. Sun and the board of directors have determined that SunSenior Corporation must revise its growth strategy to be more focused. The purpose of this project is to come up with a change plan to allow SunSenior to grow more quickly and efficiently than in the past.

Change Team Leader(s) Name—Title	Background
Jim Sears—AVP Finance	Jim Sears, the assistant vice president of finance, will be the change team leader. Jim has been with SunSenior for 5 years and has more than 20 years' experience in the industry.
	He was involved in creating the existing growth strategy and is seen as becoming a top leader of SunSenior Corporation in the future.

Change Team Members—Department	Role	Background
George Williams— Finance	Manage project finances. Determine financial models for the growth strategy. Act as a liaison between the change project team and finance.	George has been in the finance department for 2 years. He recently completed his MBA in finance and is recognized as a "do what it takes" player. He is known for putting in extra hours to complete projects and is seen as creative in making things happen and getting things done.
Karen Snow— Marketing	Provide market demographics and data to the change team. Provide past analysis of the market and future trends. Determine marketing strategy.	Karen has been in marketing for 6 years. She has been a project manager on new print and multimedia campaigns. She works well in new and unstructured environments, which aspects of this project may involve.
Bill Withers— Operations	Provide analysis of the change and the difference between current, day-to-day operations and postchange operations. Conduct analysis on capacity and staffing requirements. Take responsibility for training employees based on the change initiative.	Bill has been with SunSenior for more than 20 years. He knows how the organization functions. He has been responsible for a number of change initiatives that have led to cost savings and higher-quality service.

Table 5.1, continued

Overall Change Goal

To determine the best overall growth strategy to allow SunSenior Corporation to become the leading senior healthcare provider in the United States.

Related Goals

Create a blueprint facility model that can easily and cost-effectively be replicated.

Create a relationship plan to work with other organizations and industries that support the senior healthcare market (medical facilities, senior services, and political organizations that affect and provide services to seniors).

Define a hiring strategy to ensure that the right (caring, dedicated) individuals are brought in as part of the SunSenior approach to senior care.

Change Management Additional Requests

Date: January 1, 2011

Requestor: Dan Data—Director of IT

Description of Change Request: Have the project include an analysis of what new computer technology (hardware and software) will be required to support the change in growth strategy.

Change Team Response: The change team believes this is an important component of the overall change project and should be included. Someone from IT will be needed to analyze the current IT system and determine the difference between what exists and what will be necessary under the new growth strategy.

This person is expected to be needed between February 1, 2011, and March 1, 2011.

Stakeholder	Input	Position
Board of Directors	Wants growth.	Advocate/Supporter
Bill Daly— Operations	Needs to have a plan to manage any change in the operating model. Feels what exists today works and that it is best to stay with current strategy.	Reluctant
Dan Data—IT	Does not feel the current system can support the growth and its requirements.	Against a change. Wants an overall upgrade of IT systems before any change initiative is considered.
Donna Davis— Marketing	Definitely feels the time for growth is right.	Advocate

Progress Measurement and Control

The Growth Strategy Change Plan project is scheduled to last 90 days. Its estimated start date is January 1, 2011, and completion is expected by March 31, 2011.

A weekly status report will be shared with the project sponsor. This report will include:

- a description of areas identified as important in the change process—for example, the ease of change, cost—and how critical to the overall success of the project each area is

- any findings that can have a major impact.

After each 30-day period, an update to the board of directors will be provided, to share the progress and answer any questions that result.

Goal Setting

Setting goals keeps individuals focused on what they want to achieve, providing a means to measure progress. From a change perspective, goal setting can occur at the organization, team, and individual levels. Goals can be short term (less than a year), intermediate (1–5 years), or long term (longer than 5 years). What does the organization, team, or individual want to achieve within a certain time frame?

In setting goals, it helps to break down a large goal into manageable parts. Whether you are taking on a major organizational change initiative or a personal improvement plan, breaking down a goal into manageable tasks makes it easier to measure and achieve progress. For example, consider earning a college degree. If looked at from a bottom-line goal perspective, taking four years to complete 40 courses seems like a daunting task, but setting a goal to take five courses each semester is more manageable. Progress can be measured, and interim success can be celebrated.

In setting goals, keep in mind the other parameters, besides time, that can affect them. What are your goals with regard to money, available resources, and competition with outside change initiatives?

Depending on the type of change you are implementing and how it affects the organization, you may want to set goals in a time frame spanning anywhere from a few weeks to a few years. When crafting your goal statements, remember to make them SMART: Specific, Measurable, Achievable, Relevant, and Timely.

A poor goal statement might be "We want to greatly increase our business as soon as possible. I can use the new technology we have purchased to help." When considering potential problems with this goal statement, ask yourself the following questions:

- Is it specific enough? Does it address who, what, where, why, and how?
- Does it have a set of measures to determine progress and success?
- Is it achievable? This probably depends on how you define "greatly increase our business" and "as soon as possible." Furthermore, does it help others know when the expected level of success has been achieved?
- Does it have a defined time frame? Are milestones identified, and is there an overall completion date?
- Is it relevant to people in the organization and what they do?

A better alternative would be "We plan to double the number of customers in the over-65 age category by providing at least 10 educational seminars related to aging at senior centers over the next six months."

The difference here is that the goal is specific: "double the number of customers in the over-65 age category." It has measures and, depending on the product or service, is achievable; even more important, it gives specifics. This goal statement ties directly to today's work and how to grow it, and the six-month time frame establishes parameters to follow.

Once you have established your goals, get executive input and buy-in on the strategic priorities for the organization.

Strategy-Building Tools

You can implement either force field analysis or scenario planning to help you develop your change strategy and create your change plan.

Force Field Analysis

In looking internally at an organization's capability and externally at changes in the marketplace, one useful tool is force field analysis, which helps to identify the forces for and against change. Identifying these forces helps clarify what actions need to be taken. See Figure 5.1 for an example of this model applied to a particular change topic, global expansion, which is listed in the middle. On one side, the forces driving the change are listed using arrows of varying length to show the direction and strength of the force. On the other side, the forces resisting the change are listed, and the arrows point in the opposite direction to show resistance. Again, the length of the lines shows the strength of the resisting force.

Areas that often emerge as forces of change include

◆ political interests
◆ technological capabilities and limitations
◆ stakeholder power
◆ fear of loss
◆ opportunity for rewards
◆ pressures on performance
◆ competitive pressures
◆ customer demands
◆ availability of resources
◆ culture and tradition
◆ other change initiatives currently under way.

An alternative approach is called "enablers and inhibitors." List the change to be dealt with and ask what would enable your organization to make this change and what is already in place. Then list what could potentially inhibit the change (see Figure 5.2).

FIGURE 5.1

Force Field Analysis

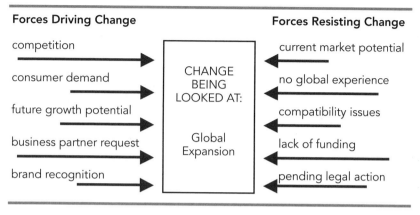

Forces Driving Change		Forces Resisting Change
competition	CHANGE BEING LOOKED AT: Global Expansion	current market potential
consumer demand		no global experience
future growth potential		compatibility issues
business partner request		lack of funding
brand recognition		pending legal action

Keep in mind factors that may not have existed before. Remember that external changes can affect the current change process. For enablers, look at things like capabilities of the Internet, especially the new functionality with social media and other aspects of Web 2.0, not only use of cell phones but also integration of personal digital assistants (PDAs) and standardization of global processes. Even the adoption of English as the world's business language can make a difference. For inhibitors, look at what people no longer accept, such as environmentally damaging processes, command and control management, and geographically isolated markets.

FIGURE 5.2

Enablers and Inhibitors

WHAT IS THE CHANGE WE ARE LOOKING AT?

ENABLERS	INHIBITORS

Identifying the right stakeholders and getting their input in the process generally helps point out issues up front and can result in a deeper level of buy-in from those involved.

Scenario Planning

Scenario planning, used often by military planners and increasingly by a number of organizations, looks at potential events and their impact. It takes a long-term view. One of the organizations most often cited as using scenario planning effectively is Royal Dutch Shell. Both Arie de Geus (1997) and Peter Schwartz (1991) from the team at Shell have written extensively on the approach, which includes the following steps:

◆ **Identify the potential drivers for change**—For Shell, an example would be the Organization of the Petroleum Exporting Companies (OPEC).

◆ **Evaluate the drivers for patterns in how they make an impact**—Shell, for example, would see how various countries respond to a new OPEC concept.

◆ **Identify the potential scenarios and the possible impact**—Shell would consider the impact of the OPEC concept on its operations.

◆ **Come up with potential strategies based on the scenarios identified**—Shell would determine what to do (have a plan ready) in case of OPEC concept implementation.

The overall goal is to identify potential opportunities and the consequences that would occur should the organization not act in the direction of change (de Geus, 1997).

In his work at Shell, de Geus not only looked forward, he also looked back at business history and found that certain characteristics stood out for those companies that managed to adapt through changing times:

◆ a strong sense of community

◆ a tolerance for change

◆ a focus on changes in the world around them

◆ financially conservative values.

Peter Schwartz uses the "what if" approach when working with his clients to help them create a response to potential changes.

Key Points to Keep in Mind

Strategy provides the detail to execute on the vision and to effectively carry out the change plan.

◆ Keep in mind the impact change will have on your organization and what it is known for. Think of the kind of business you are in—will it be the same business once you implement your change?

◆ Address what change will mean to your organization's relationship with its customers. Will your customers remain the same, or will your change allow you to serve your existing customers in a new way and to serve customers you have not had before?

◆ Consider how the change will affect the way you work and its impact on structure and processes.

◆ Consider how this change initiative will affect your competitive position: Is this the beginning of a larger ongoing change process or a one-time change event?

◆ Think about how this change fits with the trends in the industry, society, and customer base. Will your change strategy allow you to stay ahead of the change curve, or might you have to change again in the near future?

◆ Consider the overall value proposition this change will allow you to offer.

WORKSHEET 5.1

Project: Growth Strategy Change Plan

This worksheet helps to keep track of the tactical components of your change plan—the specific tasks to be completed, including functional areas, names assigned, and deadlines to be met.

Task	Individual Responsible	Due Date	% Complete	Comments/Issues
A. Project Planning and Monitoring				
1. Review/refine change plan.	Project Manager Executive Sponsor	Weekly	Ongoing	
2. Type and distribute minutes.				
3. Manage team documents.				
4. Track and resolve issues.				
5. Establish structure/times for communicating progress to sponsor(s).				
6. Update project dashboard and status report.				
B. Interviews				
1. Determine what information is needed.				
2. Build a set of interview questions.				
3. Determine people to interview.				
4. Schedule interviews.				
5. Conduct interviews.				

6. Summarize data.		

C. Identify Change Management Needs

1. Identify organizational constraints and risks and create a plan to minimize their impact on the project.
2. Identify success factors/strategies for managing change and plan to positively leverage them to the desired change.
3. Identify "Change Champions."
4. Identify key stakeholders and those who will be affected by changing from old to new process.

D. Benchmarking

1. Identify industry trends.
2. Identify fast movers and why.
3. Determine if any changes in government or politics will have an impact on future direction of operations.
4. Determine what technological innovations are making a difference.

E. Consolidate Data and Recommend Action

1. Identify trends.
2. Identify constraints.
3. Evaluate resources/capabilities that exist, or that would be needed to take action.
4. Make recommendations.

STEP 5

WORKSHEET 5.2

Strategy Checklist

Use this checklist to make sure your organization's change strategy covers all the necessary elements.

- ❑ Do we have a mission statement explaining why we exist?

- ❑ Do we have a vision that addresses where we want to take our organization?

- ❑ Are our goals—the "how" as well as the "what we want to accomplish"—clearly defined?

- ❑ Do our people understand the mission, vision, and goals and their role in making change happen?

- ❑ Do we have a way to communicate information to others and receive feedback?

- ❑ Is our strategy defined and shared so individuals know how we will accomplish our goals?

- ❑ Do our people understand the strategy and their roles in it?

- ❑ Is there a mechanism for them to have input and question it?

- ❑ Do we know what resources are available and where to get them and from whom?

- ❑ Are individuals assigned to roles with clearly identified tasks?

- ❑ Is there a way to stay in touch with individuals to gather their ideas and address their issues?

- ❑ Are processes in place to (a) address individuals' concerns along with forwarding and escalating them to the proper departments and (b) provide these individuals with feedback in return?

- ❑ Are there ways to reinforce and reward goals accomplished and efforts made in the right way? Similarly, are corrective procedures in place for not getting results or getting them in the wrong way?

- ❑ Are there ways to train and mentor individuals to help them succeed?

- ❑ Are contingency plans in place if needed?

- ❑ Should any other items be addressed in this checklist?

STEP **5**

Win Support

OVERVIEW

Who are your
stakeholders?

Interviewing stakeholders

Knowing how to influence

Key points to keep in mind

We must become the change we want to see.

—Mahatma Gandhi

Change is scary. Even relatively small changes like implementing a new software program organization-wide can cause anxiety in employees as it may directly affect their job performance. Huge changes, such as merging organizations, will cause that anxiety to multiply exponentially. To successfully manage change, you need to understand how the various groups and individuals see change and how it will affect them. If members of a group see that a change can benefit them, work with them to make it happen and garner their support. If a group is threatened, identify its leaders, keeping in mind that a person's title may not be directly linked to the amount of power or influence he or she has over the group. Finding the leaders and addressing their concerns will help sway the entire group.

Who Are Your Stakeholders?

Change initiatives succeed or fail because of people. A stakeholder matrix, as shown in Table 6.1, is a good starting point in identifying these individuals and the positions they support.

The matrix for your project may be a little different depending on what your change project entails. Some other stakeholder groups that are frequently affected include specific departments, business partners, suppliers, and groups in locations where business is conducted. The change team is considered a stakeholder group since the change directly affects the actions and future of members.

Evaluate your stakeholders and place them into one of the following categories:

◆ **Supporters**—These are the individuals and groups that generally support the change initiative.

TABLE 6.1

Stakeholder Matrix

Stakeholder	Role Responsibility	Background
Customers	Define needs	Need input from customers to determine what to produce: product, service, output of change initiative.
Organization members	Identify capabilities and make changes	Conduct day-to-day operations. Can provide input on what works and what does not. Will end up implementing changes decided on.
Sponsors	Provide resources	Have goals for change. Provide resources to get things done.
Management	Control resources	Need management to coordinate activities and initiatives between the functions working to make the proposed changes.
Change team	Determine what needs to be done and how	Need to work with all stakeholders to get things done. Coordinate activities and manage relationships. Responsible for making the overall change effort successful.

- **Detractors**—These are the individuals and groups that are openly against the change or how it is being accomplished.
- **Undecided**—These are the individuals and groups that have no opinion or are waiting for more information before making a decision.

Within each of the categories, you will find a level of support or resistance. It is important to identify this to know where and to what degree you will run into resistance or support. It also helps in building a strategy to leverage or influence each group.

The Supporters

Leverage your supporters to help you accomplish tasks and convince others to get on board with change. Depending on the level of support, they will help you to varying degrees.

The Disciples include individuals who are committed to the cause. They believe in it personally and will try to influence others to support the change. They may not have all the skills personally to get the job done, but they try to bring others together by convincing them that the change is right. They focus on the future, are confident, and maintain a sense of determination.

With the Disciples, you can openly share any resistance you run into. Sharing the issues and pointing out the Detractors may inspire the Disciples to use their contacts and relationships to convince others of the benefits of change. The Disciples may also be able to bring the Undecided to the side of the change initiative. Relationships count for a lot and can often help you face the challenges involved in the change initiative. Individuals want to work with others they trust and know won't hurt or take advantage of them.

The Believers are those stakeholders who want the change to happen and will support it, but will not openly try to convince others to change. Though they can be relied on for support and often provide resources to help make the change happen, the Believers will not take a public stance to promote it.

Change leaders should leverage the resources the Believers can bring to the change initiative, whether money, manpower, supplies, or equipment. All of these resources can be used to help drive change.

The Workhorses are actively involved in making the change happen. These supportive stakeholders do all they can. They believe in the cause and have the skills to make the change happen. They work hard, but do not necessarily try to convince others to support the change. They put in the effort and are willing to do whatever it takes to accomplish a goal. They like to be out front and are willing to take risks to produce results.

Try to provide the Workhorses with all the resources possible to do their jobs. The Disciples can further motivate this group to focus on success and overcome any challenges that arise.

The Undecided

The Undecided may not have anything against the change initiative; they may simply be uninformed or just have not paid much attention to what is going on. Here is where some marketing can make a difference.

The Masses are the majority group that is comfortable with the status quo, preferring stability to change. These stakeholders are willing to go along, but just do not know why they should or how to help. They are often unaware of the environment and make decisions based on rumors or the existing status quo. They have a hard time understanding the reason for change, but they can be convinced that it will benefit them.

Showing the Masses how the change will positively affect them can cause a large number of individuals to actively support the initiative. This strategy is often used in political campaigns. Individuals and groups are told how change will benefit them in order to get their support. As a position gains momentum, others don't want to be left behind, so they get on board. They may not know all the specifics, but because others are joining in, they want to as well.

The Lost are those supporters who just go along without knowing or caring about change. They focus on what is there, just getting by, putting in only minimal effort, waiting for the years to pass until the situation changes or until retirement comes along. Also known as "stragglers," these stakeholders want to see what happens to others before taking any action. They want to stay in their comfort zone and push back on change.

Similar to the Masses, the Lost need convincing before they will support a change effort. They do, however, present more of a challenge than the Masses because they are preoccupied with other issues. Convincing the Masses to support a change initiative can bring more of a return since the Lost are often unorganized and do not care about others' actions or events in their environment.

The Detractors

It is especially important to know why certain groups or individuals are resistant to the change initiative and what it will take to win them over or at least minimize their interference.

The Detractors are those individuals who purposely want a change effort to fail. They are happy with the status quo and what it brings them. They have the greatest fear of change, and often try to convince others that the change is bad without any substance behind their argument. They create an environment of frustration and depression, often bringing down others around them.

Ask why the Detractors are against the change initiative. If they won't talk to you directly, see if other members of the change team can provide some insights. Resistance is often based on fear of the unknown. Taking the time to understand these fears can go a long way toward addressing individuals' concerns. See Step 8 for specific ways to overcome resistance and other challenges involved in initiating change.

STEP **6**

Interviewing Stakeholders

By identifying the various groups, and in some cases subgroups, that can affect the change process, you can determine their potential concerns and how they might see the change affecting them. Checking to see if they understand the goals and why change must happen for the greater good will give you a feel for how much support or resistance you may run into. You will also better understand if these are minor concerns for the group or major issues. By being open and giving people a chance to voice their concerns, you identify yourself as a go-to person and build your credibility. Knowing the group members and their concerns provides you with a base of information that will help you understand how they may react to certain events. Getting to know the various stakeholder groups and addressing their concerns as you go, rather than waiting until an event happens, sets the tone for an open and collaborative environment.

Try using an interview process to see where key stakeholders stand and identify their personal interests. I take a funnel approach in getting individuals to share their thoughts about the effort and to evaluate the extent to which I can count on them for help.

By starting with a broad general question and then funneling it down, you will get a perspective on how the person sees change from a big picture down to their role in it. Don't be surprised if they take some of the questions in a different direction. It is OK. This will show you what is important to them and how they may respond to certain issues if and when they come up.

The funnel approach to questioning stakeholders begins with asking broad, general questions, such as "What do you know about the change initiative?" At this level, individuals talk in general terms, which is a good place to start, an icebreaker. The next step involves asking stakeholders questions that have been narrowed down, such as "From a financial perspective, what do you see as the advantages and disadvantages of the change initiative?" This level allows you to identify some specific areas that need to be addressed. Ask direct questions of stakeholders, such as "How do you see this change initiative affecting the organization's profits over the next three quarters?" At this level, you will be able to extract detailed information to be used in the change initiative.

Some other sample questions to ask include the following:

◆ Do you know what we are trying to accomplish with this change initiative? This helps to evaluate whether stakeholders have the correct information about the change effort.

◆ What do you think about the proposed changes? This helps to gauge whether stakeholders think the change is a good idea and to indicate whether or not they will be supportive.

◆ How important do you think this change effort is to the organization? The answer will help determine where stakeholders stand and how much help or resistance they will provide.

◆ Do you think this change effort will work? Why or why not? This gives a feel for stakeholders' insights and if they will help in the change effort.

◆ How do you see your role in the change effort? This direct question helps to evaluate stakeholders' view of their role and possibly match it to what is expected of them.

◆ What do you feel you can offer? This direct question serves to see what knowledge, skills, and abilities stakeholders feel they have to offer.

◆ Who do you feel will be key to have on our team? Who do you see as team players, allies, and enemies? This gets perspective on individuals' feelings about others and how they may interact.

Steps to successfully manage stakeholders include the following:

◆ Identify the various stakeholder groups and subgroups. Assess their relevance and potential impact on the change process. Are they needed to make the change effort a success? Can they stop the change effort from succeeding?

◆ Understand their interests and concerns. Can these issues be easily addressed, or will addressing them affect the overall change effort?

- Acknowledge that you understand their position. You do not necessarily have to agree with it, but you must understand it and how it may be affected by the change.

- Build a channel of communication with these groups to give you a method to deliver your message and one that also allows them to voice their concerns. Continually reach out to these groups and monitor their reaction to the changes as the process takes place, and be sure to check if they prefer face-to-face, phone, email, video (one-way, two-way), document (charts, graphs, test), or social media contact.

Having a process in place will enable you to influence your stakeholder interview and ultimately its level of success, and knowing the positions and perspectives of those around you allows for the development of an influence plan to help you manage groups of stakeholders and their interests.

Knowing How to Influence

Once you have identified the various stakeholder groups and their concerns, you can begin the process of getting them to visibly support the areas they value and to privately address contested areas.

In trying to influence individuals, keep in mind a concept known as "head, heart, hand." The basic premise is that if you can change the way people think, you can change the way they feel, which will affect how they act.

In working on a change initiative, also look at why individuals try to influence others. Often you will find unofficial alliances where the relationships are more important than the actual work. In looking at how individuals try to influence others, ask if it is for their own personal interests or to benefit others. I often find what I call the "politician" in an organization, an individual who tries to get power to influence others, not necessarily for his or her own direct benefit, but to help others in the organizational environment. This is sometimes difficult to pick up on, but it is something to be aware of since individuals can call in favors to get things done. These influence-based relationships can play a significant role in whether an initiative will have a chance regardless of whether the change initiative is the right or wrong project for the organization.

Key Points to Keep in Mind

Recognizing the supporters, detractors, and undecided gives you a starting point in creating a strategy to work with them. Ask yourself the following:

- How do you segment your stakeholders into groups and goals?
- What is it your supporters like about what you are trying to achieve?
- To what degree will your supporters back the change you are trying to make?
- What is it your detractors do not like about what you are trying to achieve?
- What would it take to win over your detractors, or at least neutralize them?
- Is there an influence strategy that needs to be put in place to address the various stakeholder groups?

WORKSHEET 6.1

Scope Change Request

Requested By: _____

Date Requested: _____

Description of Change: _____

_____

_____

_____

_____

_____

Purpose: Use the Scope Change Request worksheet when a stakeholder or group of stakeholders wants to add additional items to a change project, which can affect a number of areas. Costs can increase, time to complete may increase, and resources not originally allocated may be required. Keep in mind that any change can impact the original project and its goals.

Internal Analysis (to be completed by change team)

What impact would this change request have on the current project?

Cost: _____

_____

_____

Schedule: _____

_____

_____

Deliverables: _____

_____

_____

Recommendation: _____

_____

_____

Note: Depending on the organizational structure, the change project manager will discuss the scope change request with the executive change project sponsor.

STEP 6

Communicate Effectively

It is in times of change that leadership is required most.

—General Colin Powell

Change leaders need to be experts in dealing with people. Effective communication is a must, as is a firm understanding of your organization and its culture. Employees will want information, answers, and reassurances. In today's workplace, this is complicated further by the need to communicate effectively with a diverse range of individuals and cultures.

Do You Have the Ability to Communicate Effectively?

As a change leader, one of your most important skills is the ability to communicate. Remember, communication goes two ways. Not only must you be able to get your message across, you also need to listen to and understand the communication of others.

A good starting point to keep in mind is the level of communication a person or group needs. Too little communication may cause individuals to wonder what is missing. They may not be capable of performing their job function or may perform it incorrectly by trying to fill in the missing information with their own interpretation. Too much communication may cause them to miss the most important points. They may not do the right things, or they may assign a priority that is different from what is intended. Consider what you need from such individuals or groups. Do you want to build their understanding or cause them to take action? The levels of communication include the following:

◆ **Awareness**—This level requires only a surface-level understanding of the information being addressed, but to know where to go for details and from whom.

◆ **Understanding**—This indicates knowing about and being able to understand how things work.

◆ **Input**—At this point, you want individuals to get involved and to not only understand but be able to respond and give input.

◆ **Action**—You want individuals to take action based on communication they have received.

Also be aware of the levels at which individuals are listening to you. Do they understand your message? Are they engaged? Could they repeat back to you what you said? Sometimes asking questions helps to check the extent of their engagement; refer to Step 6 for how to interview stakeholders at all levels.

Creating a Communication Strategy

An overall communication strategy should be built for any major change initiative. The strategy should include all the appropriate stakeholders and be based on the reason for the change initiative, the goals of the change initiative, the roles and responsibilities of individuals involved in the change process, and a way for them to have a voice. Openness, honesty, and sharing of updates should be the underlying principles behind the strategy.

The basics of creating a communication strategy include determining the goal of your message. While you may know what you want to say and how you want others to react, it may not come across so clearly to others. Start by encoding your message, or determining how you believe recipients will understand it. Then decide how you will transmit the message. What medium will be most effective in getting your message out and your point across? Is your message a simple one, or will you need to cover a number of points in detail? Finally, how can recipients ask for clarifying information or provide feedback?

Medium

Your communication strategy should include the method of communication. As technology has developed, it has both positively and negatively affected communication. Determining what channels to use can be as important as the message itself. See Table 7.1 for some guidelines on choosing your communication medium.

TABLE 7.1

Communication Channels

Channel	Advantage	Disadvantage
Face-to-Face	Two way, can adjust and alter message as needed based on reaction of listeners.	Takes time and costs more than other channels.
Cascaded Face-to-Face (one individual to a group, that group to a large group, that large group to the next group until everyone in the organization has been reached)	Gives direct contact with everyone. Shows a chain of communication. Provides a two-way opportunity to allow individuals to ask questions. Gives a sense of inclusion.	Message may get altered as it goes from level to level. Success may depend on the individual delivering the message.
Broadcast Video/ Recorded Video (e.g., YouTube, Vimeo)	Can reach a large audience, give them visuals to go with message.	One way, not everyone may have the necessary technology to see.
Social Media (e.g., blog, wiki, community of practice site)	Allows everyone to comment and participate.	May lose control and the purpose of the original message may be altered to take things in a different direction.

Table 7.1, continued

Channel	Advantage	Disadvantage
Email	Quick, cheap, can reach a large audience.	Don't know how long it will take for the person to open the email. Impersonal, leaves the meaning of the message to the reader and his or her interpretation.
Phone (direct)	Speak to a person directly and can address issues in real time.	Very costly and time-consuming.
Phone (indirect)	Voice mail blasts can reach a large audience quickly.	Don't know when message will be received. Cannot directly respond to a listener's questions.
Newsletter (paper or electronic)	Can connect with the masses fairly quickly.	One way, and if there are issues with the articles, it takes time to follow up.
Letter	For those who grew up with this as the primary medium, it may provide a level of comfort.	Slow, expensive (postage and materials). Updates take too long to get out.
Combination of media	Can be effective if the proper mix is selected. Matching the right media with the right audience is key.	Can be ineffective and costly if the mix does not meet the audience's needs.

Audience

It is also important to keep your audience in mind. A brief message is best. Link to more details if necessary, but provide a summary that covers the main points. Check to make sure the message is clear. Can it be easily understood? Is it better to focus on the qualitative or the quantitative, or a combination of both? Remember the higher up you send a message in an organization, the less chance the recipient will look at it unless it has an attention-grabbing point. Along with this, the credibility of the source is important. Do others respect this source? If not, find a sponsor to forward the message with an endorsement. Is the message compelling? Why would the receiver care about the message or take action as a result of receiving it? Does the message need to be altered to the different stakeholder groups receiving it? Is the change message compelling enough to get the receiver to act? These are small points, but they can make a difference in whether communication succeeds or not. Understand what success looks like. Can you define and measure it?

Keep in mind whether you are communicating with a group or an individual. Communication to an individual may be more effective in one way than communication to a group or an entire organization. Add in the global organization and the challenges that go with different geographical regions, and the communication effectiveness factor increases. Also keep in mind the organization's structure. Communicating to a group that is organized around product lines is different from communicating to a group that is industry aligned or matrix designed. Deciding what messages go to which groups helps clarify how each should be communicated.

Getting and Using Feedback

Not just about "speaking," communication involves "listening" as well. In some cases, listening means monitoring the environment to see what issues and challenges people are facing. In others, listening means proactively seeking input for ideas and suggestions the organization should consider. In still other situations, listening means receiving and acting on feedback from earlier communications.

When soliciting feedback, change leaders must genuinely listen for understanding, not just for an opportunity to respond. They should let all individuals finish their thoughts and try not to be judgmental. The point here is not necessarily to agree with them but to understand them—and to be able to acknowledge that you have heard what they have to say.

Change leaders may choose to arrange face-to-face meetings specifically to allow for stakeholders to provide feedback. Feedback from employees can also be gleaned from regularly distributing a newsletter that allows readers to send in comments or submit their own stories. In other cases, surveys can be used to solicit specific input. Internet tools such as SurveyMonkey (www.surveymonkey .com) and Zoomerang (www.zoomerang.com) make the posting and retrieval of survey data much easier than in the past. In other cases, a simple suggestion box can be used to allow individuals to give their input.

In addition to providing everyone with an opportunity to make comments and provide feedback regarding the change initiative, you must address the comments and deliver your response to the appropriate individuals. Today an organization can easily put something like a blog in place as a communication channel. Also remember that not everyone may have access to all media, so it is important to determine how individuals in an organization get their information. You may have to use multiple channels: bulletin boards, mailings, emails, and so on. When using open media, such as a blog, plan for responding to inappropriate comments (will they be removed, ignored, or commented on directly?).

Responding to feedback is important; if done correctly, it can help increase support for the change effort. Ignoring feedback can negatively affect, and even eliminate, support.

Evaluation of the feedback should therefore be a priority. How do individuals' suggestions realistically fit in with the project? Answering this question can help you determine whether it can be incorporated and, if so, conduct an analysis of its potential impact. Project completion time, cost to incorporate, and available resources are a few things to keep in mind.

Showing individuals they have a voice and that leadership cares about what they have to say does a lot to strengthen the culture of an organization.

Addressing the cultural aspects also goes a long way to helping you as the change leader understand the environment and identify supporters and detractors and why. Check to see if you need to focus on the change effort itself or the organization's reaction to the change initiative; this will help you determine what type of approach to take.

Communicating Across Cultures

If you work in a global environment, it is important to understand the culture, customs, and behaviors of your co-workers. U.S. customs and courtesies do not always work well in other parts of the world, and in some cases, what is considered an acceptable way of doing business in other parts of the world is looked down on by U.S. culture.

If your change initiative is global in nature, note that many studies have examined differences in cultures and how to work with individuals from other cultures. Some of the most recognized work is from Geert Hofstede (2001) on what he calls "cultural dimensions." He points out that going into another country and trying to do business like we do in the United States can lead to misunderstandings and bad decisions. In his work, he looks at five dimensions and their ratings in different countries. A website that provides a number of related interactive tools is www.geert-hofstede.com.

Being aware of different cultures can make you more effective in working with them. On the softer side, consult *Kiss, Bow, or Shake Hands* (Morrison & Conaway, 2006), a book that has some good hints and tips, along with its companion website: www.kissboworshakehands.com.

STEP 7

An Example of Global Understanding

I remember my early and sometimes embarrassing encounters with Japanese businessmen—and at that time, they *were* all men. We Americans would come into a meeting, quickly flip our business cards across the table, and start talking about our products and services. The Japanese would start by individually presenting their business cards vertically and bowing. Each then provided such personal details as where he went to school.

After the introductions at one particular meeting, things went from bad to worse. We presented our objective, with the Japanese often nodding and saying "hai" (which we translated as "yes"), and we felt very confident we had just made a deal. In follow-up discussion, however, we found we were wrong. By nodding and saying "hai," the Japanese were acknowledging what we said and that they understood, but were not necessarily agreeing with us.

From a U.S. perspective, we had been making a transaction. From a Japanese perspective, they had been building a relationship—something to keep in mind when you and your organization are preparing to communicate with individuals from a different culture. Cultural relations have come a long way, but this gives you an idea of the challenges involved.

Key Points to Keep in Mind

Communication is often the make or break factor in the success of a change initiative.

- ◆ What is the overall goal of communicating related to this change initiative?
- ◆ Are stakeholders targeted and to what degree: to inform, to get input from, or to drive action?
- ◆ Does the communication plan address the who, what, when, where, why, and how?
- ◆ Have you asked stakeholders if they have a preference in how they are communicated with?
- ◆ If the project involves global coordination, have the customs and courtesies of others been addressed?

WORKSHEET 7.1

Building a Communication Strategy

In completing this worksheet, other groups the change manager may consider include customers, business partners, representatives from particular company divisions and locations, investment analysts, and employees—anyone who will be affected by the change initiative or who is necessary to make the change initiative a success.

With whom do we need to communicate?	Why do we want to communicate with this individual/group? (What is our purpose: to inform, educate, or move to action? What do we want to happen as a result of our communication with this individual/group?)	What do we need to communicate? (And at what level do we need to communicate: executive summary, overview, or detailed analysis?)	What is the best way to communicate with this individual/group? (Note media and frequency.)	What to keep in mind? (Is there anything unique involved in dealing with this individual/group?)
Examples				
Executive Sponsor	• Keep him or her updated on progress and issues.	• Summary-level accomplishments. • Details about issues.	• Weekly email. • Face-to-face contact as needed.	• Very hands-on and detail-oriented.
Investors	• Keep them informed of progress. • Maintain their continued support in the change effort.	• Progress and the value the change initiative will bring the organization.	• Formal, quarterly report. • Investor relations.	• These are the individuals who own our stock. They are looking for information about the return on investment of our change initiative.
Stakeholders (This category can be broken down into various stakeholder groups for specific communications, but here is general information for all.)	• Keep their support. • Count on them for resources for the change initiative.	• Project progress, milestones achieved.	• Weekly newsletter (online).	• In the newsletter, need to provide related change project information. • Have a frequently asked question section. • Have a column from the change leader with details of what is happening.

STEP

7

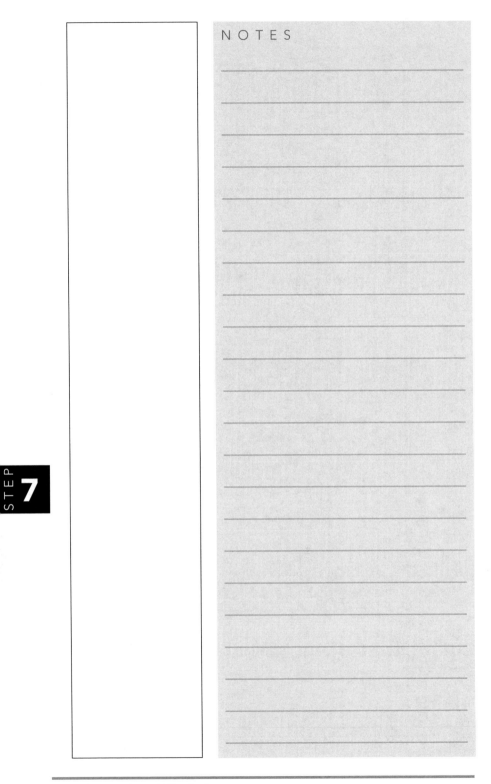

Overcome Challenges

OVERVIEW

Why do people resist change?

Reasons for resistance

Stereotypes, groupthink, and other things that get in the way

Addressing resistance to change

Key points to keep in mind

Change will only happen when the pain of change is less than the pain of staying the same.

—Richard Beckhard

During a change initiative, challenges come in a number of ways and from a number of sources. Some result from events you expect or know may happen. For example, people quit their jobs, leaving you to come up with substitute resources, or competitors come up with new products that threaten your market share. Other challenges arise more unexpectedly. For example, the whole team leaves the organization at a critical point in the project, leaving you with no way to complete your mission or forcing you to allow a competitor to take over your company. Being able to deal with challenges has become a routine part of every function in an organization. Understanding how to address issues and knowing how to utilize resources makes a difference in the overall success of the individual and the organization. This section covers a variety of challenges that you may encounter and gives you some tips for overcoming them.

STEP **8**

Why Do People Resist Change?

Don't expect everyone to stand in line waiting to join you as you embark on a change project. Individuals become comfortable in their routine. While some employees may not like their current situation (and even complain about it every day), they know what to expect, which is less scary than the unknown that change brings. Individuals may resist change even when they know the future brings opportunity. In fact, some people are so reluctant to change that they may resist even if they know that the consequences of not changing would be dire. They just ignore, deny, or hope that things will work out. The sad fact is they rarely do.

Individuals give many reasons for resisting change (Schuler, 2003). The challenge in the change process is to understand and overcome individuals' reasons for resistance. Some are simple and based on misinformation; others are deeply rooted in values and tradition. The degree of risk people see in a change is based on their perception, not necessarily on actual reality. Sharing information and having an open channel of communication between those initiating and those being affected by the change can make a difference in the level of success in both the individual and the organization.

Schuler gives the top 10 reasons individuals resist change:

1. The risk of change is seen as greater than the risk of standing still.
2. People feel connected to other people who are identified with the old way.
3. People have no role models for the new way.
4. People fear they lack the competence to change.
5. People feel overloaded and overwhelmed.
6. People want to be sure the new ideas are sound.
7. People fear hidden agendas among those driving change.
8. People feel the proposed change threatens their personal level of confidence.
9. People fear a loss of status or quality of life.
10. People genuinely believe that the proposed change is a bad idea.

The root of resistance is often a lack of understanding what change is needed and why. Educating individuals can jump-start their understanding of the need for change. Showing them the anticipated positive impacts of change and the probable consequences of not changing can further drive the point home. Relating the organization's position to that of its competitors also serves to emphasize an organization's reason for change (Pritchett, 2009).

For example, although it was once a major Fortune 500 company, computer maker Digital Equipment Corporation (DEC) no longer exists because its founder and CEO resisted the idea of the personal computer. He was well known for saying that "there is no reason for any individual to have a computer in his home." Just think of the market he missed with this type of thinking! The ability to anticipate and take advantage of change is key to an organization's continued viability.

Often an organization's bureaucratic structure can cause problems. Bureaucracies generally provide structure and routine and give people methods and processes for completing tasks. The problem is they become entrenched and can get in the way of change. People who are afraid of change often go back to the rules imposed by bureaucracies to defend their actions and their resulting resistance. Expose resistance when you can. Bringing the issues into the open for people to address shows no one is trying to hide anything. Whether the issues are real or not, the commitment to address them shows everyone you have nothing to hide. This demonstrates commitment from leadership and openness to ideas and input from all members and levels of the organization.

STEP **8**

Helping people "get it" is an important step. Resistance to change increases when people don't understand why change is happening. Ambiguity leads to uncertainty, and as a result, people slow down and tend to do nothing. Change needs a purpose to get people to commit. Goals help clarify people's responsibilities and give them something to set their sights on. Letting them know the anticipated challenges and problems sets the tone and prepares individuals for potential hang-ups. People need to know what change means specifically to them. The potential rewards that accompany success and the consequences of failure provide a context for acceptance of change.

We all have stories of how individuals have dealt with change. Many are filled with details of the rise and results of resistance. Signs of resistance include:

- ignoring direction
- not using identified processes and procedures
- not being willing to learn a new system
- challenging change (both overtly and covertly)
- openly criticizing the new processes and procedures
- finding excuses for not fulfilling responsibilities
- sabotaging initiatives.

Also keep in mind that resistance from employees is a form of feedback from people with knowledge and experience about an organization's daily operations. Treat their concerns as valuable information, and you can gain ideas on potential challenges and opportunities as well as develop insights on how to communicate the change initiative to them (Ford & Ford, 2009).

Reasons for Resistance

Lack of Trust

A major factor in getting individuals to go along with change is the level of trust they have in those initiating it. If they have experienced unsuccessful or dissatisfying changes in the past—for example, leaders failed to provide expected support, or made promises that never came true—there may be reluctance. The credibility of the people driving the change is a key factor—if individuals see change managers as trustworthy, they are more likely to receive a message about change with enthusiasm.

Though not an easy measure, the trust factor is a major component in overcoming past challenges in pursuit of change. Relationships based on respect and trust can overcome hang-ups based on disagreement on process and procedure. Individuals want to know that they will not be taken advantage of or made to look bad. When people trust each other, they are more willing to share, take on greater risks together, and strive to achieve more overall.

Some specific actions that change leaders can take to build trust include the following:

- ◆ Build a common frame of reference. This involves communicating with others so they know why the change initiative is taking place and what it will bring.

- ◆ Provide a person and place to go to when issues come up. Often when individuals are undergoing a change process, they cannot rely on their traditional support system to provide them with answers. Providing a "change champion" or change office they can go to for answers to their questions helps build a common bond. They need to feel they can approach this person or group without fear that they will be looked down upon or retaliated against. A blog or similar tool can allow individuals to ask questions so the change team can respond and share information.

- ◆ Create a common experience. Training is often part of the change process, and smart change leaders realize it actually serves two purposes. One is to teach individuals to do things in a new and different way. The second and often overlooked purpose is to "socialize" individuals to the coming change. Those who participate in training not only receive a set of skills, but a collective insight and frame of reference for going forward.

STEP **8**

Peer Pressure

Individuals may wait for their colleagues and co-workers to respond before deciding how to act themselves. In some cases, they would never listen to the ideas of a specific individual or group, but when it comes to the unknowns of change, they look for consistency in others' response.

To combat this type of resistance, change leaders need to communicate that, though relationships may work differently after implementation of the change, individuals are being given an opportunity to affect their own future by participating in the change initiative. Leaders need people to participate in making change happen, not just wait for it to happen to them.

Finding and working with those who are looked up to by others can help get resistant individuals on board. If those in whom they already have the trust the change team is trying to build choose to support the change initiative, the resistant tend to follow along.

Opposition to Outside Influences

This type of resistance occurs specifically in organizations where an outside consultant or firm has suggested or designed the change initiative. It happens because organizations are reluctant to try ideas or new approaches not developed in-house, particularly when they have been successful on their own. When ideas or examples come in from other firms, they are often rejected before even being considered. Organizations need to ensure their culture does not block out ideas from outside sources or those not considered part of the mainstream organization.

When working with outside organizations, it helps to introduce them to everyone involved in the change initiative, including those who will be affected by the change. Sharing their background and what they see as their role, how they can help, and what they have done for others can help build credibility and open up others to work with them.

Self-Doubt

Challenges may come from how individuals feel about themselves and their ability to change. Often self-doubt and a fear of failure drive an individual's reluctance to change more than the organization's change initiatives. People may question whether their skills will work in the changed organization.

Helping individuals understand their role in the changed environment and showing them how they will be able to function whether through training, implementation of new processes, or changes in organization structure can go a long way toward laying the groundwork for individuals overcoming their self-doubt.

Initiating training and getting individuals involved in new processes, along with giving them the opportunity to work with new equipment early on in the change initiative, can help individuals feel more comfortable with it. Have mentors or skilled individuals on hand to provide advice or guidance to those who want it. These mentors can share hints and tips related to what is stated will work and "what really works" behind the change process.

Some individuals may be more open to getting involved than others. These change team members may take on the role of active change agents, and as a result, others may look to them for help in changing. When individuals are willing to serve as change agents, provide them with the tools and training necessary for success. Highlight their efforts and reward their successes. Give them visibility. It will encourage them to continue and show others that the changes can succeed. Pilot programs to get more individuals involved in a less risky environment also help reduce individuals' lack of confidence in their ability to change.

Overload

Day-to-day operations often need to continue during the change process. Requiring individuals to work on both the current operations and the change initiative can lead to frustration and burnout. Not just a problem for individuals at the rank-and-file level, the risk for overload is often more critical for managers who are responsible for both maintaining current operations and implementing the change initiative.

Overload can also affect individuals trying to learn and perform at the same time. Often with change comes unsuccessful and unplanned events. Sometimes alternatives are readily available, and other times no contingencies have been planned for. Frustration results, and individuals' behavior often turns to denial and blame.

Ways to address overload include looking at the change project schedule. Is the work being shared equally? At some point, one individual may have more assigned tasks than others. Check if those who are not as busy can cover even simple tasks (getting supplies, drafting documentation, responding to simple inquiries) to free up those who are heavily involved and under pressure to meet deadlines. Small tasks may seem small, but all tasks take time.

Related to overload is fatigue, another factor complicating change initiatives. Individuals often want to do a good job, but if processes are not well defined, they do everything by trial and error, which takes a great deal of time and mental effort.

By definition, a change initiative is a project with a designated start and end date, and intermittent milestones and deadlines. When a project starts to fall behind schedule, project managers often request more resources. The challenge, in the case of supplementary people resources, is the additional time needed to train them, another cause for overload.

Filters and Biases

One of the more openly addressed but least understood issues is that of bias. Biases come from a number of experiences and values developed over the years. The best way to deal with them is to realize they exist and deal with them directly.

As the change manager, you may come across the following types of bias in individuals who are resistant to change:

- ◆ **Historical Bias**—Judging things and individuals because of lessons learned in the past. Sometimes this type of bias is the hardest to overcome, especially if a change effort conflicts with an individual's upbringing and value system.
- ◆ **Leniency Bias**—Tending to be more lenient toward or accepting of a certain change over another.

- **Severity Bias**—Tending to judge or resist a certain change more harshly than another.
- **Central Tendency Bias**—Treating all change efforts the same. This can be a problem if an actual change does need to be addressed in a certain way for a certain reason.
- **Primacy and Recency Bias**—Judging individuals involved in the change initiative by their first or latest impression.

The information people receive goes through filters, whether they are based on individuals' learning and past experiences or messages received from others. Television news programs provide a clear illustration. Fox and CNN, for example, may tell the same story, but the persepctives, reasons, and even some facts behind the story may vary greatly between the two networks.

It is important for change managers to ensure that not only change team members but all individuals potentially affected by the change know and are able to confirm the facts about the change initiative and then make decisions accordingly. Too often individuals choose to resist change based on limited information.

Hoarding Information

Those organizations whose culture focuses on sharing of information usually experience less resistance to change initiatives. Other organizations in which all members look out only for themselves and have no incentive to help each other are very slow-moving toward change.

To build cohesion among members of the organization—and thus combat the type of resistance that occurs when individuals hoard information that would, if shared, benefit everyone in the organization—change managers should encourage competition between individuals in what I call a "take it to the next level approach" whereby individuals get ahead by developing skills and achieving greater accomplishments as a team. Present the change initiative as an opportunity for them to develop and get better, not to hold others back. Offer incentives for making progress as

STEP **8**

a group. The challenge is to avoid encouraging individual competition at the expense of overall group cooperation in the pursuit of accomplishing change.

A culture of sharing creates a better environment for successful change initiatives because it brings individuals together and helps relationships form and build. A great example of this is the Linux operating system for computers. When Linus Torvalds started writing the code to build this operating system, rather than keep it to himself he put it on the Internet and allowed others to contribute and improve it. With no financial reward involved, this process gave the individuals who participated in the change a sense of belonging and accomplishment. It drove others to add what they could to make things better.

Stereotypes, Groupthink, and Other Things That Get in the Way

The number of potential challenges in a change effort is limitless. The following influences may give some insights to how individuals in various roles look at others in the change process. Some may sound a little extreme in terms of organizational change, but recognizing and being able to address related situations can make the difference between success and failure.

- ◆ **Stereotypes**—Preconceived, oversimplified, exaggerated, and often demeaning assumptions of the characteristics possessed by an individual due to his or her relationship to a specific group. Prejudice involves prejudging a person's qualities and value based on arbitrary characteristics such as race. Problems occur in organizations when the work assigned or even an opportunity presented is based on assumptions rather than abilities. Change managers can overcome stereotypes by getting to know individuals instead of automatically categorizing them with a certain group.
- ◆ **Ethnocentrism**—The tendency to evaluate other ethnic groups according to the values and standards of one's own

ethnic group, especially with the conviction that one's own ethnic group is superior to the other groups. Individuals who take an ethnocentric approach to others miss the opportunity to take advantage of diversity in accomplishing a goal.

◆ **Xenophobia**—The fear or hatred of strangers or foreigners or of anything strange or foreign. While especially extreme in regard to organizational change, I have seen xenophobia in cases of mergers and acquisitions, where an almost xenophobic atmosphere surrounded any newcomers. Building exercises, along with opportunities for groups from the various organizations to get together and learn about each other as people, can help in this situation.

◆ **Megalomania**—An excessive preoccupation with one's own importance; the feeling that one is better than others and all things should focus on the individual and his or her goals at the expense of others. Everyone has likely worked with a megalomaniac at some point. The challenge is to get such individuals to realize that by helping others they are in fact helping themselves.

◆ **Groupthink**—A situation in which individuals give in to the pressure of others in spite of knowing an issue or problem exists. One of the most in-depth studies of groupthink is related to the Space Shuttle *Challenger* disaster. An engineer knew issues existed with what is known as O-rings at certain temperatures and that those issues could lead to disastrous results to the shuttle, but gave in to pressure from others on the team, who were more concerned with their reputations and maintaining their set time line.

◆ **False beliefs**—Beliefs based on folklore, tradition, or simple misunderstandings that have no substance behind them. Individuals' beliefs and values affect how they respond to a change scenario. Some values are deep-rooted and difficult to change.

◆ **Habit**—The status quo. Sometimes individuals do things a certain way just because they always have. The issue comes in when these habits are challenged and by whom.

Often told in illustration of the last point is the humorous story of the pot roast and why the ends are cut off. A couple is preparing a pot roast for a holiday meal. Prior to putting it in the cooking pan, the wife cuts off the ends of the pot roast. Seeing this, the husband asks her why she cut off the ends. She replies she isn't sure, but her mother always did it that way. So the husband asks his mother-in-law why she cut the ends off the pot roast, and she says her mother had always done it so she did it too. So he asks his wife's grandmother why she cut the ends off the pot roast, and she explains that her cooking pan was too small to fit the entire roast.

Just think how much pot roast—or time to make progress toward positive change—has been wasted over the years because of a lack of understanding.

Addressing Resistance to Change

Always remember to utilize your change vision to help people understand the reason behind and goal for the change. A little planning for potential challenges and an established mechanism for two-way communication can stave off resistance before it starts.

General strategies for addressing resistance to change, along with potential advantages and disadvantages of each approach, are presented in Table 8.1. Also, there are two particular responsibilities of change managers in addressing resistance—handling disagreements and building coalitions.

Handling Disagreement

Disagreements will come up in any change project. They key is to use the differing opinions to generate new and potentially better

TABLE 8.1

Strategies for Dealing With Resistance

Approach	Potential Advantage	Potential Disadvantage
Ignore	Not giving attention to the issue may make it go away.	The issue may become larger and more difficult to overcome if not addressed immediately.
Inform	Providing information and educating individuals on what is happening may eliminate their resistance and inspire their buy-in.	It may give the resisting group more information to strengthen its point of resistance.
Dialogue	Direct conversation with individuals and groups that are resisting change can allow for an exchange on the issues and how to possibly resolve them.	Dialogue acknowledges that an opposing group exists whose issues are enough of a concern to be addressed. This could lead to the resisting group gaining more power.
Confront	Direct confrontation can address issues openly and show that the resisting individual or group has no substance behind its resistance.	If the resisting individual or group gets the attention of the general population, it may strengthen and reinforce its claim that there is an issue.
Discredit	Addressing the source of the resistance rather than the issue can discredit the individual or group. Depending on the past record and credibility of the individual or group, this may be an approach worth taking.	Attempting to discredit an individual or group may bring sympathy from others in the organization. It may also be seen as a less than ethical attempt by the change team to thwart resistance.

STEP 8

ideas to deal with a situation. Mary Lou Higgerson (1996) has come up with a helpful set of ground rules for working through the process of disagreement:

◆ Take charge and show that things like abusive language will not be tolerated.

◆ Derogatory comments that represent personal attacks will not be tolerated.

- Differences of opinion will be discussed, and everyone will be heard.
- Individuals will be able to express their views without interruption or fear of retaliation.
- Unsubstantiated assertions will not influence the vote or outcome.
- Issues, not personalities, will be subject to debate.
- Tears or emotional outbursts will not derail discussion of substantive issues.
- Department issues will be discussed and decided at department meetings, not at any subgroup level.

Bill George makes the good point that "crises offer rare opportunities to make major changes in an organization because they lessen the resistance that exists in good times" (Lagace, 2009).

Building Coalitions

Building coalitions can often help in overcoming challenges to change. Coalitions bring groups together to support a common purpose. They are generally formed temporarily and among groups that would not normally be business partners but in this case are trying to achieve a specific common goal. Their success is driven by the personal relationships built between representatives of these groups. Building a reputation as a coalition builder can also help individuals make progress career-wise.

Essential to creating a coalition is ensuring that the values of your organization are visible, not just in words, but in the actions of members and participants sponsoring and leading the change initiative. A set of core values gives individuals in an organization a guideline for how to behave and on which to base their decisions.

Forming a coalition takes individuals with insight and the ability to bring groups together in pursuit of a common interest. A potential pitfall in being part of a coalition is that portions of one coalition partner's goal set or principles may be opposed by another partner, or certain provisions may not go over well with other organizations with which yours has a positive relationship. Change leaders realize that what one group wants may not be exactly what another group wants, but both groups' goals may be similar enough that working with each other can help them both make a positive change. Coalition builders look for an overlap of interests and the potential impact on two groups in a partnership.

An example of a coalition coming together involves the Organization of the Petroleum Exporting Companies (OPEC), which keep oil prices artificially high because, as a group, they have the power to do so. The countries may disagree on a number of other issues, but when it comes to the price of oil, they all want to keep the price high.

In addition, a common language helps individuals in an organization to understand the meanings and implications of events. Just about every profession, industry, or organization uses a unique language to describe itself and how it accomplishes its goals. Accepting a language from the past can cause challenges while building one for today, keeping in mind the external environment, can bring individuals together and act as a means of bonding.

Note that coalitions of opposing sides can develop as well. A number of groups that don't have much in common outside of one specific cause might come together and then drive another set of groups to come together, again to support a single view, but this time in opposition to the first coalition's stance. In some cases, partners in one coalition can be opponents in another. For the purposes of addressing resistance to change, consider if any individuals, groups, or organizations can help your organization overcome potential barriers to change, and how to best work with them. In working with coalition members:

- Look for common areas of interest.
- Consider the strength of the overlap in these areas of interest.
- Identify neutral areas, or areas that will not be affected by any position a coalition partner takes.

- Identify areas of disagreement and how critical they are to your position.
- Determine the consequences of not getting your way.
- Decide whether you can give up some of this in order to get support for your main goal.
- Look again for areas of common interest that you might build on to form a stronger coalition.

Key Points to Keep in Mind

It's impossible to anticipate all the challenges that will spring up during your change initiative, but by understanding some of the tools, concepts, and processes outlined in this chapter, you can take steps to overcome group and individual resistance to change.

Asking yourself the following questions can help you avoid the major challenges a change initiative presents:

- Who are the various groups that may be affected by your change initiative?
- What do the various groups have to gain and lose as a result of the change?
- How much power do the groups involved have, and how might it affect the change effort?
- What actions are groups or individuals taking? Are they resisting the overall change initiative or only certain aspects of it?
- What resources do you have should a group put up resistance to the change you are initiating?
- Have you planned for contingencies in case an issue comes up or things don't go according to expectations?

WORKSHEET 8.1

Reflecting on the Past to Prepare for Future Change

This exercise is intended to help individuals identify some issues and surface concerns that they might encounter in embarking on a change initiative. Keep in mind it is also about possibilities.

1. Take a moment to think about a change initiative you were previously involved in.

   ◆ Was it successful or not?

   ◆ What were some of the factors leading to the success or causing the failure?

   ◆ Were the right people doing the right things?

   ◆ Was there a support system in place to help individuals through the process?

   ◆ Were there any warning signs or indicators of issues?

   ◆ What else was the change dependent on?

2. Then attempt to work through potential solutions and contingencies.

   ◆ Are there any similarities between the previous change initiative and the current one? If so, what specific issues relate to the current initiative?

   ◆ Do any other things come to mind that the change team needs to be aware of?

   ◆ How should you address these issues? Should you address them up front or have a contingency plan?

   ◆ What is the best way to communicate your approach?

STEP **8**

WORKSHEET 8.2

Measuring Change Resistance

One of the challenges of change is to identify the source and extent of resistance. Change team leaders can give this 10-question assessment to members in the organization at early stages of change and during the change process. The goal is to get an idea of where potential issues are coming from and why, and whether or not they have been effectively communicating the project and its goals. It can also help identify specific ways to develop further support.

1. Can you identify the goals of the change initiative?

No				Somewhat			To a Great Extent		
1	2	3	4	5	6	7	8	9	10

2. Can you identify the executive sponsor to the change initiative?

No				Somewhat			To a Great Extent		
1	2	3	4	5	6	7	8	9	10

3. Do you feel your job will be better as a result of the change initiative?

No				Somewhat			To a Great Extent		
1	2	3	4	5	6	7	8	9	10

4. Have you had the opportunity to provide any input on the change initiative?

No				Somewhat			To a Great Extent		
1	2	3	4	5	6	7	8	9	10

5. Were you informed that the change process was going to take place?

No				Somewhat			To a Great Extent		
1	2	3	4	5	6	7	8	9	10

6. Have you been kept informed of the progress of the change initiative?

No				Somewhat			To a Great Extent		
1	2	3	4	5	6	7	8	9	10

7. Do you know the members of the change team?

No				Somewhat			To a Great Extent		
1	2	3	4	5	6	7	8	9	10

8. Do you know when the change initiative is scheduled to be completed?

No				Somewhat			To a Great Extent		
1	2	3	4	5	6	7	8	9	10

9. Do you feel the change initiative can be successful?

No				Somewhat			To a Great Extent		
1	2	3	4	5	6	7	8	9	10

10. Do you believe this change initiative is necessary?

No				Somewhat			To a Great Extent		
1	2	3	4	5	6	7	8	9	10

Change Input Scale:

Score of 80 and above = Indicates there is a good job being done in communicating the project and its goals.

Score of 60–79 = Indicates there is some understanding, but there may be more support available with some communication.

Score of 40–69 = Indicates increased communication about the project and its goals is needed.

Score below 39 = Indicates a serious lack of understanding on the part of members of the organization. Action needs to be taken to get the word out.

STEP

8

Measure Success

OVERVIEW

How do you measure success?

The measurement process

Key points to keep in mind

If you can't measure it, you can't manage it.

—W. Edwards Deming

Measuring and evaluating the success and results of your change initiative is vital. Knowing what data to look for and how to interpret it is key to knowing whether you are on the path to success or failure. Often, organizations decide on a set of measures for their change initiative that have no relation to true performance. These measures focus on activity rather than productivity. An example would be interviewing 50 stakeholders to understand what they hope to see as a result of the change initiative, only to have them come back and say they do not like what they have seen. The focus should not be on interviewing 50 stakeholders—it should be related to how the stakeholders see progress toward reaching the goals agreed on at the beginning of the project. Measures need to give you information you can use to show progress toward a goal.

Measurement is important for a number of reasons:

◆ It allows for communicating the level of progress toward reaching a goal.

◆ It keeps stakeholders informed of what is working and potential issues that have come up.

STEP 9

- It shows investors the return on their investment.
- It allows others to conduct their change plans to work in conjunction with yours.
- It allows concerned parties to provide feedback according to what they see.
- It provides an opportunity to make changes or corrections to the plan.
- It acts as a learning tool to show others what works.
- It allows an organization to build a culture of sharing.

How Do You Measure Success?

Helping your stakeholders identify and agree on areas to measure, and how often to measure them, builds credibility and allows them to see how things are actually progressing compared to the change plan. It allows for issues to be addressed early on before they turn into major problems. It also allows for contact on a regular basis, which is another important aspect in communicating with stakeholders to build strong relationships. Make sure your metrics are aligned with the goals of your change initiative.

What will you be measuring? How will you be measuring it? How often will you share information on progress toward the goals? The answers to these questions should be agreed to by both the stakeholders and the project sponsors. Any changes in plans or time line should be discussed and have their buy-in. Keep areas in mind that refer to quality, speed, and cost, sometimes referred to as the "better, faster, cheaper" model. Some areas to consider incorporating in your measures include the following:

- **Budget**—What budget was set for the project? How is the money being spent (burn rate), in what amounts, and during what period of time? Measures would show whether the change initiative is under or over budget and by how much at what point in time.
- **Other Financials**—How much will the change initiative save in production? From an internal perspective look at cost cutting, and from an external perspective consider revenue generation. Can you see an increase in existing

customer spending or new customers coming onboard as a direct result of the change process?

- ◆ **Time**—What time line did you set before starting the change project? Identifying key project dates and specific project milestones gives individuals involved in the change initiative something to strive for as they make progress toward change.
- ◆ **People**—How have the skill sets of change team members affected other areas of the project and the overall goals? Measuring individuals' contributions makes it easier to know what areas are lacking and what type of additional change team members are needed to fill these gaps.
- ◆ **Recognition**—How are change team members responding to the change process? Are they excited? Is the project acting as a motivator to drive further change, or do members of the change team need more support?
- ◆ **Quality (Thoroughness)**—Are there recognized industry standards that can help in the measurement process? To what extent and in what ways has your organization adhered to these standards?
- ◆ **Functionality**—Can the results of your change initiative be measured incrementally as you work to achieve your overall goal? One way to measure progress is to release a subset of a product line as it is completed, but before the whole product line is available.
- ◆ **Resources**—How effectively are you using available resources, and to what extent? Consider enlisting technology, knowledge, and other tools or supplies.
- ◆ **Competition**—Are you keeping up with, ahead of, or behind the competition?

Keeping stakeholders informed of the progress toward reaching the change goals is important in maintaining their ongoing support. It is best to identify what will be measured, how, and how often at the start of the change effort, in your change management plan (see Step 5). A good plan gives stakeholders an opportunity to provide ongoing feedback from their perspective as well.

The Measurement Process

All of the above areas can be measured in a number of ways. When measurements are made during the change process, it is known as formative evaluation. This type of evaluation is done at regularly scheduled periods or at certain stages of a project and is recommended for organizational change.

Among the many terms and concepts used in the measurement process, the concept of performance measurement attempts to look at performance in terms of outcomes—such as the number of parts produced per day or financial performance for the quarter—and inputs—such as the amount of raw materials, the quality of the material input, and the skills of individuals involved in the process. The key is to use measurement to follow your progress toward your goal. Taking action on a small issue can save a project from much costlier problems down the road.

Kirkpatrick's Levels of Evaluation

Closely related to individuals' performance are the training and development they receive while participating in an organizational change initiative. One model often used in the process of assessing individuals' experience is Kirkpatrick's Levels of Evaluation (Margolis, 2009).

The model is based on a continuum from how individuals feel about the training they have received to whether any results can be derived from that training. Level 1 looks at whether participants enjoyed the initiative. It is often not enough to affect what they do. Level 2 looks at learning. Individuals can be tested to see how much they have learned. Level 3 involves making observations to see if individuals behave differently. Level 4 is the most revealing, but also takes the longest time to measure. It considers whether things have improved from an earlier state. An added challenge in Level 4 is making sure any changes can be linked back to the training. A fifth level has been proposed to measure the return on investment from the training. Basically, did the money spent on training pay off?

STEP 9

Remember that measured success in one change area may be offset by an issue caused by change in another. Take, for example, the case of a well-known computer company that, for years, received high marks in customer service. In an effort to cut costs, the company outsourced much of its customer service department, but this action, while drastically reducing costs and achieving the company's goal by any standard of cost reduction, caused the reported quality of its customer service to decrease dramatically.

One customer's online comment demonstrates the extent of the decline: "On my last purchase, the monitor was DOA [dead on arrival]. I called the customer support number and got a guy with a very heavy accent who directed me to the monitor manual on CD, provided with the computer. I asked him if he understood the irony of putting the monitor troubleshooting guide on a CD since if the monitor didn't work you'd have no way of reading the guide. After 40 minutes of being on hold and talking to a supervisor, they said they'd have to send a new one—the very suggestion I'd made at the beginning of the call."

Key Points to Keep in Mind

In the end, a measurement system should
- link to the goals of the organization
- provide feedback as to the effectiveness of the organization's strategy
- be easy for individuals to understand
- look at areas relevant to what is being measured
- look at both short-term and long-term performance
- be consistent with the reward structure of the organization
- be a constant, not just an occasional activity
- give insight into not only what is wrong but also how it could be better.

WORKSHEET 9.1

Areas of Change Initiative Measurement

A change project generally has one primary goal. If subgoals are also included, it is helpful to complete multiple versions of this worksheet and look for consistent areas of measure.

CHANGE PROJECT GOAL (primary goal)

AREA OF MEASURE[1]	STANDARD OF MEASURE[2]	VARIANCE (positive/negative)[3]	REASON FOR VARIANCE[4] (if negative, include plans to improve)

1. **AREA OF MEASURE:** Consider what would help indicate whether the change initiative is moving along successfully—for example, financials, time, deliverables, stakeholder feedback, and team motivation and development.

2. **STANDARD OF MEASURE:** Consider historical standards, industry standards, the actions of competitors, and predictions for your industry.

3. **VARIANCE:** Consider the difference, both positive and negative, between what you are getting and a standard of measure.

4. **REASON FOR VARIANCE:** Consider the reason for a variance so it can be adjusted for if needed.

Review Lessons Learned

OVERVIEW

What areas should you review for lessons?

Sharing lessons learned

Key points to keep in mind

That's the reason they're called lessons, because they lessen from day to day.

—Lewis Carroll

Reviewing the lessons learned during a change process is important for the change manager. After participating in a change initiative, managers will benefit from looking back at the transition period from prechange to postchange to review what they've learned, as well as what worked or didn't work, and to think about how they will approach their next movement toward organizational change. Managers are encouraged to take the time to consider how the outcome of one change initiative will affect their future behavior in the organization, especially in change management.

What Areas Should You Review for Lessons?

Lessons can be gleaned from a number of practices and processes involved in initiating change. In reviewing a particular experience

STEP **10**

with change, managers should look out for ways they might improve in the following areas:

- ◆ **Process (how things get done)**—As a result of something that happened during action toward change, did you discover how to make any processes necessary for change better, faster, or cheaper? Was the strategy clear in how to execute the change process? Did the processes work as planned, and if not, how did your expectations compare to what actually happened? It is a good idea to document the impact (in terms of time, money, morale, and so on) of not being able to follow the process as planned. In retrospect, would you have done something differently, and if so, why? Consider "other possible options" and why each would be worth looking at in future change initiatives.

- ◆ **Technology**—Did the technology support go as planned? Identify the issues that could have been avoided, such as not having the right equipment in place at the right time or a lack of access to the information team members needed because they could not get a security clearance. Differentiate these from actual technology problems; for example, was the online search tool you used effective for the type of research you were doing? Did your system have enough bandwidth capacity to download the large amount of video needed to be reviewed by the remote team in Asia? The prior easily could have been addressed by having the right processes in place. The latter possibly would not have been known but, as a result of what you are doing in documenting lessons learned, will help in future change initiatives. Also, considering the pace of technological change, document whether there are any new technologies that could be used. Are there ways to apply existing technology that emerged as part of the change process and could improve on current change practices? Look at it from the perspective of what existed and what could have been utilized to make a difference (that was not) and whether there was anything that was used that had a positive impact on the overall project (saved time, saved money, improved quality, and whatever else it is that is used as a measure of effectiveness in your organization). Secondly, be sure to examine from the perspective of new innovations in technology that have emerged since the change initiative was started, and that future change initiatives should consider.

◆ **Employees**—Were the right people selected to be on the change team? Should you have used any different criteria in making your selections? Were the team size and the scheduling of people on and off the change project the most effective? Did you end up running into conflicting schedules, and what possible suggestion would you have to do differently? Is there a better way to utilize these "people resources"? Do they need training prior to the next change initiative? When and in what ways did they work most effectively, and where is there room for improvement?

◆ **Customers**—If you worked directly with customers, what was different from what you expected as part of the original change plan? What impact (positive or negative) did it have on the change project? Did you learn to work with customers in any different ways (cooperating, collaborating, partnering)? How are customers, and their needs, changing? Have you developed certain capabilities that can help them in new ways? How effective was your communication with them (content, media, frequency, feedback capability)? What prechange ideas played out, what really happened, and what could have been done better?

◆ **Competition**—How did the output of your change initiative position you against your competitors? Was it what you had planned? Why? Are your competitors doing things differently? Have you gathered any ideas for gaining and maintaining a competitive advantage over them, or to search the public media channels for information about them? From a lessons learned perspective, what other change initiatives should be undertaken to further enhance your position in the competitive marketplace? Give

STEP **10**

the details of what, why, and how it would make a difference, and how the lessons learned can position you to be more effective.

◆ **Other**—Have you found anything else as a result of this change initiative that can help your organization be more efficient and more effective? It can be related to people, process, technology, innovation, or even something that has not been identified to this point.

In each of the above areas, be sure to reflect on the goals that were set, to what degree they were accomplished, and how they were accomplished. What happened as compared to what was supposed to happen, and why were there any differences? The point is to determine what should be done to correct things in the future.

Sharing Lessons Learned

Capturing, reviewing, and especially sharing lessons learned with others can make the difference between an organization succeeding and ceasing to exist. By addressing what works for a change initiative as well as what does not, an organization can become more agile and responsive to the challenges of change. Leveraging the knowledge that goes with lessons learned allows an organization to change more quickly and with less expense. According to a study by the Project Management Institute, Fortune 500 companies lose more than $31.5 billion each year because they do not share knowledge (Logue, 2004). In addition to the money lost, learning what went into overcoming a challenge helps individuals become better and encourages them to be more innovative.

Make it easy for members of your organization to understand the information they need in order to be more successful in their next change initiative. This will allow them the knowledge on which to base future change-related decisions. The lessons learned by managers as part of the change process is important to share with all stakeholders so they don't repeat your mistakes and so they do take advantage of the things you did well.

Key Points to Keep in Mind

◆ Collect lessons learned along the way, for example, by keeping a journal. Waiting until the end often results in lessons not being contributed, or if they are, their facts can be distorted.

◆ Take time to reflect on any problems, issues, and so on that happened and why. Could the problem have been noticed earlier? Were there any early signs or warnings? Given that this is a time of reflection, would you have done anything differently?

◆ Remember to pass along things that went well. Success-ful processes should also be collected. Having a standard that works well can save time and money up front in the change process.

◆ Also comment on alternatives tried and results from them. They can often provide guidance on change initiatives similar but different from this one. What alternatives did you look at, which did you try, and why?

◆ Did you look at or have any contingency plans? Did they come into play? Why or why not?

STEP **10**

REFERENCES

Collins, J. (2001). *Good to Great*. New York: Harper Business.

de Geus, A.P. (1997). The Living Company: A Receipt for Success in the New Economy. *The Washington Quarterly 21*(1): 197–205.

Ford, J.D., & Ford, L.W. (2009). Decoding Resistance to Change. *Harvard Business Review*, April: 99–103.

Higgerson, M. (1996). *Communication Skills for Department Chairs*. Bolton, MA: Anker Publishing.

Hofstede, G. (2001). *Culture's Consequences: Comparing Values, Behaviors, Institutions, and Organizations Across Nations*. Thousand Oaks, CA: SAGE Publications.

Lagace, M. (2009, October 13). *7 Lessons for Navigating the Storm: Q&A with William W. George*. Retrieved February 16, 2011, from http://hbswk.hbs.edu/item/6214.html

Logue, A.C. (2004). "20/20 Foresight." *PM Network*, 18(9), September: 32–38.

Margolis, D. (2009). *Don Kirkpatrick: Father of the Four Levels*. Retrieved March 5, 2010, from http://www.clomedia.com/profile/2009/November/2791/index.php

Morrison, T., & Conaway, W.A. (2006). *Kiss, Bow, or Shake Hands*. Avon, MA: Adams Media, an F&W Publications Company.

Prahalad, C.K. (2010). Why Is It So Hard to Tackle the Obvious? *Harvard Business Review*, June: 36.

Pritchett, P. (2009). *Resistance*. Dallas, TX: Pritchett LP.

Project Management Institute. (2011). *Knowledge Center*. Retrieved
   January 20, 2011, from http://www.pmi.org/Knowledge-Center
   .aspx

Schuler, A.J. (2003). *Overcoming Resistance to Change: Top Ten Reasons for Change Resistance*. Retrieved September 25, 2010, from
   http://www.schulersolutions.com/resistance_to_change.html

Schwartz, P. (1991). *The Art of the Long View*. New York: Currency
   Doubleday.

INDEX

George Vukotich, PhD, is the Department Chair of the Graduate Program in Training and Development at Roosevelt University. Since joining the university, he has been involved in expanding the program to include a global presence. In addition to his academic work, George has more than 20 years of experience in the corporate and consulting field working for organizations such as IBM, Accenture, and BP. His work  includes implementing a number of major change initiatives, developing and executing organizational strategy, and working to develop corporate leaders. Lieutenant Colonel Vukotich has also served with the U.S. military, leading a number of training initiatives. His previous book, *Breaking the Chains of Culture—Building Trust in Individuals, Teams and Organizations*, focuses on helping individuals be more successful by developing a culture of trust.